SPAIN:

The Glory and
the Tragedy

By the same author:

The Struggle For Madrid, 1958

Spain and Vietnam, 1968

El Asedio de Madrid, 1970

AIMS HISTORICAL SERIES NO. 7

The American Institute for Marxist Studies (AIMS) is a non-profit educational, research and bibliographical institute. Its purposes are to encourage Marxist and radical scholarship in the United States and to help bring Marxist thought into the forum of reasonable debate to produce a meaningful dialogue among Marxist and non-Marxist scholars and writers. Its policy is to avoid sectarian and dogmatic thinking. It engages in no political activity and takes no stand on political questions. It grinds no axe for any group, party, sect, organization.

To these ends it invites the support and participation of all scholars and public-spirited individuals.

SPAIN:

The Glory and the Tragedy

ROBERT G. COLODNY

Professor of History
University of Pittsburgh

Published for A.I.M.S. by
HUMANITIES PRESS
New York 1970

Dedicated to all those
who have sacrificed
so that
the Republic might live.

CONTENTS

I

"*Spain is today a sequestered nation. It cannot speak because its mouth is pressed shut by the muzzle of the censorship. It cannot write because its hands are shackled. The instinct of survival prevents the people from pouring into the streets to protest such slavery. An army oppresses the country, and it is easy for it to silence the protests of the unarmed multitude with rifles and machine guns.*"

—Vincente Blasco Ibañez,
Alfonso XIII Unmasked (Paris, 1925)

❋ ❋ ❋

Over thirty years have passed since fascist-inspired insurrection by the Spanish generals began a three-year bloodbath for the Spanish Republic. The Second World War, the inevitable sequel to the Iberian catastrophe, ended a generation ago. Civil wars, revolutions and counter-revolutions have scarred the earth since VE and VJ Days were thought to have ended the agony of bloodshed which has been the lot of mankind since the guns of August boomed in 1914. The havoc of Korea is now followed by the unending anguish of Vietnam, and Hiroshima and Nagasaki cast their radioactive shadow over all the cities of the globe.

Alerted by ancestral voices prophesying apocalyptic violence, the historical imagination faces a severe challenge. No longer does it serve any useful purpose to portray the

1

horror of war. After Auschwitz and Dresden; after Hiroshima and a thousand nameless Indochinese villages liberated by napalm, appeals to the ethical sensitivity of mankind are not apt to alter the geopolitical plans of existing power elites. Statesmen frozen into diplomatic immobility by outmoded views of the external world will regard arguments cast in archaic moralistic language as at best irrelevant to the deadly chess games now being played, wherein countries and subcontinents are mere tactical pawns in a nightmarish gambit for global hegemony. The computers of the pentagon, which can calculate the probable kill of armed peasants after a B-52 raid on a jungle village, are not programmed to evaluate the experience of past blunders—otherwise the American Secretary of State's historical experts would have to supply the electronic brains with but two symbolic names—*Lidice* and *Guernica*—to determine with considerable accuracy the folly of considering villages and towns as absolutely expendable in the pursuit of Grand Strategy.

The historian need be convinced of only one truth to make his craft meaningful in the context of today's disasters: the memory of mankind is sufficiently complete, sufficiently charged with the symbols of past political crimes, so as not to allow self-appointed guardians of human destiny to execute with impunity the same blind policies which led to boundless suffering for nameless millions during this century. The Spanish Conflict is such a symbol.

Time has not dimmed the relevance of this tragedy for today's groping generation, nor has the displacement in space of the main battlefield to Asia reduced the significance or the *universality* of the Spanish experience. The villages of Andalusia and those of Southeast Asia have this in common; they were both turned into cemeteries of the innocent in the mindless pursuit of a fugitive security against popular revolution. The dead peasants were statistics in struggles to arrest movements of mass protest against obsolete social orders. The conflict in the olive groves and wheat fields of Spain and the guerrilla war in the rice paddies of Asia have similar origins, and both reveal the terrible failure of the liberal, pragmatic imagination to free itself from the tyranny of slogans about the world and to grasp the reality of human efforts to end intolerable conditions of social humiliation.

A generation ago the Spanish Republic was assaulted and destroyed in the name of a holy crusade against Communism. Most of the arguments used against the militia columns of Republican Spain (the guns came from Moscow and Mexico) are part of the ideological arsenal of those who support the use of American power against armed Asian peasants (the guns come from Moscow and China).

As is well known, the Spanish conflict posed issues which sharply divided the governments of the West from their people. The man-in-the-street, not presumed to be an expert in high diplomacy or military strategy, saw through the follies and duplicity of his rulers, and in an unprecedented outpouring of generosity, supported as best he could the embattled defenders of Madrid; whereas the legal guardians of Western Civilization, with an ill-concealed sympathy for the crusaders against bolshevism, proclaimed neutrality and appeased the fascist Axis as the best insurance against the spread of social revolution at home and abroad.

Now the practice and purpose of the appeasement policies of the thirties is wrenched out of its historical context, and it is asserted by Harvard Deans and Confederate Senators that the guerrilla armies, wherever they arise as the inevitable consequence of village misery and despair, are to be blasted from the face of the earth, otherwise the contagion will spread. That this was the same rhetoric used by Hitler, Mussolini and Franco and echoed by Imperial Japan, then engaged in suppressing communist banditry in China, is a coincidence wisely unmentioned by the clever proponents of global counterinsurgency.

Whether they succeed or fail, counter-revolutionary wars reveal the same historic forms: the armies of intervention, if they come from societies where the ruling elites fear social change, cloak their support of conservative forces of repression behind high-blown claims of disinterested service to mankind's highest ideals. This was the case when the despotic empires of Eastern Europe invaded revolutionary France in the eighteenth century. This was the political justification of Metternich's era of defense of legitimacy in the nineteenth century. When Churchill and his associates in fourteen countries invaded the newborn Soviet state of Lenin, the motives as expressed by His Majesty's Government were pure and quite detached from the grubby interests of British Imperialism. So it was again in Spain. The support of rebel generals, feudal aristocrats, Moroccan mercenaries, Mussolini's blackshirted Fascist Legionnaires and Hilter's Condor Legion was portrayed by right-wing politicians in the West and the press lords subservient to them as a Holy War, a sanctified defense of a Christian bastion threatened by Kremlin-inspired revolutionaries.

The record shows that peoples are not always as blind and stupid as those whom providence or chance has placed in positions of power. As the author has written elsewhere, "Spain was where the common man last asserted in deeds the dignity of his autonomy and the rectitude of his conception of the way the world was going. . . . Here the old and traditional elites that have ruled Europe for centuries were confronted with ultimate questions, and like Pontius Pilate of old, turned away to wash their hands."

The common man was right then because he understood, albeit intuitively and instinctively, that the passionate resistance of the Spanish militia grew out of a desperate effort to defend a Republic which promised redress of ancient cruelties and injustices, and that the banners of the Republic were raised in a cause that was remote but universal.

The weight of German Stukas and Italian Caproni bombers eventually turned the tide against the abandoned and betrayed Spaniards and the small army of the International Brigades that answered the appeal of Madrid.

But while the flames of Spain lit up the international political landscape, the whole world went to school, learning between last rites and Axis ultimatums what the impulses were that led a generation to offer youth and life on anti-fascist barricades.

Now an Asian puppet dictator, whose avowed idol is Adolph Hitler, summons great armies to defend his regime against the revolution of despairing country folk. The parallel with Spain is clear and ominous, but this is what makes the retelling of a twice-told tale meaningful. The origins of the never forgotten war in Iberia and the new calamity in Asia are similar. The obscuring of the origins in both cases led to the confusion and political disarray of great peoples. In the case of Spain, the Axis was permitted to grow strong enough and so to conceal its ultimate purposes, that the civilized world was pounded to the very edge of oblivion until rescued by a coalition that included the armies of the Soviet Union. This is the supreme paradox that links the two epochs, that lays bare for all but the blind to see that the socialist world and that which calls itself "free" without more detailed specification are not separated in terms of human purposes by an unbridgeable abyss; that such divisions as do exist need not be filled with the corpses of peasants.

The Spanish conflict, which so aroused the conscience of a vanished world, did so not merely because of the heroism of the combatants, but because the issues of the war were only secondarily those of geopolitics, strategic bases, the testing of new weapons and tactics. Spain became the "most shattering experience of modern political life," in the words of Howard K. Smith, because the great masses of the Spanish Republic, rousing themselves from decades of fruitless political squabbling, stood in magnificent disdain of the odds against them to defend a more humane vision of how life might be organized. With the insight of Don Quixote, they wished to bury a decayed and burdensome past. Alas! the windmills against which they rode were real, steel-tipped and swastika-covered.

To recall the days and years of the war in Spain against the contemporary background of the drift toward a Third World War is an endeavor to permit the million fallen to bear witness. Each generation, of course, must make its own judgment. No generation, particularly the young of this one, dare be indifferent to the bell which tolled for the people of Spain.

II. *The Spanish Republic: Years of Hope and Violence*

The Second Spanish Republic was born on April 14, 1931. The occasion of its proclamation was municipal elections which gave evidence of great republican majorities in the major cities of Spain. The Bourbon monarchy, headed by Alfonso XIII, which had been kept alive for nearly a decade by the reasonably benign dictatorship of Primo de Rivera, disappeared without a shot being fired in its defense. Middle class republicans, and particularly socialists, after consulting the populace at the polls, proceeded to establish a government, to write a constitution, and to prepare a set of legislative remedies for the ancient ills of Spanish society.[1]

The bourgeois politicians—men of great good will and some learning, poets, orators, lawyers—men who would have been revolutionaries if their Republic had come into existence in the eighteenth century—were deceived by the momentary euphoria that followed the flight of the king and his retinue to France. Like their spiritual kinsmen of 1848, February, they believed that a fundamental reconstruction of Spain could be carried out without the violent opposition of the traditional oligarchy—church, nobility, army, high bourgeoisie—for whom the king was but a disposable ornament. They believed also, despite the obvious evidence to the contrary, that the people of Spain mentioned in the preamble to the Constitution—"the workers of all classes"— would behave as a passive chorus ready to applaud the promised reforms, touching as these did, state, church, army, the agrarian question, the status of labor, education, etc., and that both the time-table and the depth of these reforms would be left to the cabinet and the Cortes.[2]

The Azaña government was fatally wrong on both assumptions. The oligarchy, with the experience of centuries, lived in fear; the people—the overwhelming majority of them—lived in misery.[3] And thus there existed a Republic with only a minority of republicans, and though the word was magic to the liberal intellectuals who created it, it was anathema to the elites that had reduced a once proud empire to the miserable status of a backward Balkan state; who, suspicious of all social innovations since the Counter-Reformation, regarded the mild proposals of reform as a manifestation of Moscovite subversion.[4]

In quick succession Azaña and his colleagues antagonized the Church by secularizing laws, by depriving it of its educational monopoly. They infuriated the military caste by proposing the supremacy of the civilian order. They created a panic in the real owners of Spain by an agrarian reform which fed the land hunger of the landless peasants without any basic attack on problems of land tenure inherited from the time of the Carlist wars. The urban workers, whose disaffection from the old regime had been responsible for Republican majorities in the cities, were driven to sullen hostility by the draconic repression of strikes, attended by the violence traditional to such clashes of interest in Spain since the coming of the Industrial Revolution at the dawn of the twentieth century.[5]

Furthermore, the Spanish Republic had come into existence on the downward swing of the historical pendulum of democratic advance. This was the year IX of the Fascist coup in Italy; the Weimar Republic, one of the models studied by Spanish state builders, was already moribund; the brief interlude of Labor Party reform in Britain had ended in disaster; neighboring Portugal had passed from republican chaos to clerical fascism. The Great Depression, injuring profoundly a semi-colonial producer of raw ma-

Despite these massive disabilities, the Republic made an terials such as Spain, put the industrial magnates in a combative mood and deprived the country of that spirit of ordered compromise which is the alternative to violent revolution.[6]

Superimposed upon these difficulties was the fragmentization of the nation—the inheritance of geography and history. Catalonia and the Basque country, the sites of the major heavy industry, were gripped by separatist movements with mass support. These drew their inspiration and strength from the petit bourgeoisie, whereas the great figures of industry and finance were allied to the land-owning oligarchy. Thus the modernization of Spain—the true mission of the Republic—lacked the support of the classes that had in generations past laid the foundations of modern Britain, France and Germany.[7] Compounding these calamities was the fact that the most militant proletarian movement in Spain drew its inspiration not from Marx or Mill, but from the Anarchist Father, Mikhail Bakunin.[8]

heroic effort to break the crippling grip of titled and mitred parasites. Ably supported by the Socialist Party and the long silenced members of the intelligentsia, it began to tamper with the foundations of the feudal order. The result was a dress rehearsal for the oligarchy's rebellion of July, 1936.

In August of 1932, a Rightist coup, in preparation since the flight of Alfonso XIII, took place. Led by General Sanjuro, but poorly sustained by other military chieftains, the revolt was quickly suppressed.[9] The Republican leaders were deceived by the fiasco of the military putsch. They failed to realize that the enemies of the regime were closely allied to reactionary circles in France and England, as well as those in Germany and Italy. The Spanish oligarchy, amazed at the leniency with which the conspirators were treated—no death penalty, honorable exile, minimal prison sentences (compared to the brutal repression of working

class revolutionaries)—lost its fear of the word "Republic."
Could not Republics be captured from within? Could not
the great wealth of the elite weight the electoral competi-
tion against the disorganized and quarreling political parties of the Left? Had not Weimar spawned the successes of
Hitler's Nazis? Were not most of the civil servants hold-
overs from the monarchy? Did not the Guardia Civil, the
very symbol of monarchical control of the countryside, still
patrol the forgotten villages of Spain? Thus, wiser than the
middle class politicians and their Socialist Party allies, the
Spanish oligarchs moved to take over the Republic from
within.[10]

The moderate reforms passed by a Cortes dedicated to
modernizing Spain without affecting the social structure of
the nation—a social structure which institutionalized the
political control of a frightened minority—these reforms
might have been prologue to evolutionary change, slow but
sure, such as took place in nineteenth century Britain, if
the Government—Azaña and his allies—had been able to
retain the confidence and respect of the disinherited millions of town and countryside. But with the most powerful
working class force, the Anarchist CNT, dedicated to a cult
of violence, hostile to the very spirit of middle class politics,
the insurmountable crisis of confidence came early and
fatally.

Violence splattered blood from Bilbao to Sevilla. To the
burned-out wreckage of churches and convents, which had
been the instinctive response to the first monarchist-clerical
attacks on the Republic, were added dynamited trains and
pistol duels between fanatics of the political extremes. The
Government responded by closing communist and anarchist
headquarters in Barcelona.[11] Hoping for humane methods
of maintaining public order, the Government created the
Guardia de Asalto—men of proven loyalty to the Republic—
and trained supposedly to impose their orders without im-

mediate recourse to rifles and pistols, the ancient tradition of the Guardia Civil.

Then came the crime of Casas Viejas, a wretched little village of Andalusia. There, early in 1933, the local anarchists rose in revolution and proclaimed liberatarian communism for their village. In crushing this feckless uprising, a platoon of Assault Guards shot fourteen prisoners in cold blood, the partially burned corpses being left as an example to the villagers. Evidence presented to a parlimentary commission of inquiry suggested that the Assault Guards acted on direct orders of the Madrid Government. Spain, which in a few years was to be drowned in blood, responded to Casas Viejas with a reflex of horror. Was this the new order: If so, was it better than the reign of kings? It was a small affair in a land used to violence, but the Azaña regime never fully recovered from it.[12] Nor could it recover from the rapid swing towards conservatism of those members of the industrial and commercial classes who had either welcomed the Republic or passively accepted it. The pressure of working class militancy and the deepening world economic crisis drove them into the waiting arms of the old order's political formations.

The Cortes under socialist pressure had enacted a new complex electoral law through proportional representation which favored cohesive bloc politics. In the elections of 1933 the socialist-democratic-republican majority was destroyed: The Right (with a multitude of groupings) won— 212 deputies; the Center—169; the Left—89.[13] The anarchist masses, whose violence had given the pretext for the repression which smeared the Republic with "blood and mud and tears," the phrase of the centrist leader Diego Martínez Barrio, boycotted the elections and thus permitted the Right to gain legally all the levers of power in Spain.

The complex political history of Spain between the November elections of 1933 and the desperate revolt of the

Left of October, 1934, turned on one problem and one problem only: how could the Right, behind the facade of parliamentary maneuver, emasculate the Republic and cripple with reasonable permanence the twin spirits of reform and revolution fed continuously by the desperate social conditions of the masses? Mussolini and Salazar had provided one set of answers. The emergence of Hitler in January, 1933, as legal Chancellor of the Reich provided another. But the Spanish Right—the powers behind the shifting political groups represented in the Cortes—was in no hurry. Quite legally it annulled the constructive work of the first Republican Cortes. It reversed the trend towards federalism; it restored the clerical prerogatives; it halted agrarian reform; it permitted a pitiless deflationary policy in factories, mines and fields.[14]

But this did not produce the psychological certainties that besieged minorities profiting from a given social order require. Hydra-headed, the revolutionary masses remained —even as they had survived the bloodletting of Noske and the Frei Korps in Weimar Germany. In their millions they were not to be tamed by Guardia Civil or Guardia de Asalto alone.

Fascist groupings were formed in Spain as early as 1930 by Giménez Caballero. In March of 1931 Ramiro Ledesma Ramos formed a political party with the name Las Juntas de Ofensiva Nacional Sindicalista (JONS). Its program was mystical, violent, anti-Marxist, anti-middle class. Unamuno, the Spanish philosopher, called it "the offensive of retarded mentalities." The early history of the movement was indeed comical, but its design indicated a shrewd sense of Spanish realities. It recruited from the same centers that fed the anarchist mass movement. (Was not Hitler's party called the National German Workers' Socialist Party?) It constructed a program that appealed to the wounded pride of the nation's youth, capitalized on the weakness of the bourgeois mentality in Spain, and infused the program with a corporate mystique—a telling point in a nation fragmented by three hundred years of disastrous experience.[15]

In the fateful March of 1933, José Antonio de Primavera, Marques de Estella, son of the late dictator, avid admirer of Benito Mussolini and Julius Caesar, founded the Falange Española.[16] This brought into sharper focus the ill-defined plans of previous totalitarian groupings. Spain was to have a genuine revolution, but it was to be led by the Right against the Marxist Left, against the capitalist forms. A year later the competing fascist groups would merge. Copying Mussolini's early adventure in Italian blood politics, the Falange organized shock groups of armed killers and conducted a guerrilla war against the socialist and communist militants.[17]

The Falange, however, grew slowly in numbers, and the oligarchy could not count on its becoming a practical rival to the traditional mass movements. There remained the army, the officer-bloated mass of military parasites, smarting under the Azaña-inspired reforms, nursing old wounds to its martial pride across the globe and new ones inflicted by the Moroccans of Abd-El-Krim. The officer corps of the army retained as part of its collective self-image the belief that it had an historic privilege to pronounce on the right to survival of Spanish governments.[18] It had made and unmade them in the nineteenth century, and though the officers had sworn the soldier's "sacred oath" to the Second Republic, the future would give eloquent proof to the contingent nature of martial honor in Spain.

With the deepening crisis of the Republic, the broken threads of the Sanjurjo revolt were picked up by wiser hands. Union Militar Española began to weave a web of conspiracy which knit together all the garrisons of the peninsula and its colonial possessions. Strands of this web passed through Lisbon, Paris, Rome, London and Berlin.[19]

A political party, Renovación Española, ostensibly a monarchist political grouping, was formed with the express

purpose of providing a cover for the foreign links of the
would-be putschists of Spain. Into its treasury flowed
the wealth of Basque and Catalan millionaires who, like the
Ruhr and Rhine coal and steel kings of 1932, wished to lay
once and forever the spectre of Red Revolution and to end
the interminable separatist movements that raged around
the industrialized provinces of Spain.[20]

III. *Spain's Red October*

1934 was the year of no return for Spain, as well as for Europe in general.[21] While José María Gil Robles, political agent of the Jesuits and mastermind of the parliamentary cohorts of the oligarchy, maneuvered in the wings, Spaniards of all classes shuddered at the news from Berlin and Vienna. The many-millioned legions of German social democracy and communism had vanished before the Nazi and Catholic coalition, not with a bang, but with a whimper. The Marxist leadership was hauled off to concentration camps and gestapo torture chambers. In Austria the clerical fascist Dolfuss, having first undermined the legal props of the parliamentary republic, turned the cannon of the Heimwehr on the socialist workers of the capital. Austrian democracy perished in one magnificent but too long delayed spasm of proletarian heroism.

The difference between the two responses was not lost in Spain. The Right saw that the road to power in republics need not involve a violent *coup d'état*. With commanding posts in the bourgeois state, and with the connivance of traditional elites, the "Republic of all workers" could be transformed into a corporate-clerical dictatorship behind the cloak of legality. Gil Robles did not conceal his intentions. With cynical disdain of his announced victims, he proclaimed the resolve of the clerical-monarchist-rightist bloc to seize the positions of state power one by one. If necessary, he would provoke a revolution in order to have a pretext for total repression.[22]

Belatedly the Left began to stir. Aging socialist Francisco Largo Caballero, reformist and bureaucrat through generations of experience, goaded by anarchist taunts and spurred on by his younger colleagues, adopted a revolutionary stance and rhetoric.[23] The small sectarian Communist Party of Spain, moved from its obsession with clandestine activity by the Third International's representatives, began an intensive propaganda and organizing campaign throughout the country. With a Moscow trained, but solidly proletarian leadership steeped in the traditions of Spanish working class life, the small Party aspired to be a *catalyst* transforming the *attitudes* of Caballero's numerically powerful following—both in the Party and the Socialist-dominated UGT (General Workers Union).[24]

The collapse of all of the reforms of the Republic under the combined assault of the Right convinced the old socialist Counselor of State of the Rivera dictatorship that the only hope of the masses was a social revolution. Thus was born the idea of the Alianza Obrera—a united grouping of working class parties and the trade unions.[25] The Communist Party participated in the Alliance, but not the anarchists. Caballero, dubbed by his ambitious friends "the Spanish Lenin," had no conception of the requirements of a revolution—but this was what the Alliance was to conduct. The socialists smuggled arms to Asturias (hardly as many as the foreign fascists supplied to the Right), but failed to inform their allies of plans or tactics.[26] The revolution lacked a general staff, liaison committees, even a clear statement of minimum goals. It was nourished by a realization that Spain could become a fascist country through the actions of a Cortes dancing to the tunes of Gil Robles, and behind him, the untouched power of church, army and oligarchy. In early October the crisis matured. The first CEDA (Confederation of Rightists) ministers entered the cabinet.

Caballero believed that revolutions developed spontaneously from the convictions of the masses—that it was un-

Spanish to organize, to plan. On the eve of the proclamation of a revolutionary general strike that was to culminate in an armed insurrection of the workers, he broke all contact with the communists and failed to inform the anarchists of his intentions. The result was predictable tragedy. Barcelona was dominated by the army in a matter of hours. Bilbao, Valencia, the Andalusian cities, never stirred. The peasants —the great reservoir of revolution—had not been considered and were unaware of the movements taking place in their name. The rebellion in Madrid was a lamentable farce. The leadership was arrested at home or went into hiding, leaving the Castilian workers in a *sauve qui peut* mood.

In Asturias, the coal mining province of the north where in September Gil Robles had made his most menacing threats of a fascist takeover, the workers rose as one man. They had arms and above all, they had unity—a sense of proletarian solidarity that broke through the sectarian partitions of trade union or party. Now for the first time since the Paris Commune of 1871 Western Europe saw the creation of an armed workers' socialist commune. Well supplied with dynamite, obeying their own leaders with iron discipline, the Asturian miners swiftly secured their mountains and valleys and blasted their way into the towns. Unaware that they fought alone, that the rest of Spain was bound and gagged, the miners, to the cry of "Unite, Proletarian Brothers!" turned to face the full fury of the Spanish State.

The Government called two arch conspirators of Union Militar Española to restore law and order, Generals Franco and Goded. The generals, uncertain of the response of peninsular conscripts, and given carte blanche by the Republic, summoned to Spain the Colonial Army of Africa— the Foreign Legion, the Moorish mercenaries, the units brutalized by the sanguinary years of Rif warfare. For fifteen days the miners fought a desperate rear guard action and then, with 3,000 dead, 7,000 wounded, they surrendered. The repression which followed, unmatched in animal ferocity until the Nazi epoch, saw the number of prisoners, including the elite of democratic Spain, swell to 40,000.[27]

The victory of the Right appeared to be complete. The proletarian leadership was incarcerated, the militants dead or in hiding. Why not press on to the last stage of Gil Robles' plan? The very brutality of the African Army horrified that part of the petit bourgeoisie not committed to fascism. The reactionary and corrupt politicians did not want to surrender the political stage to Gil Robles, nor to monarchist chief Calvo Sotelo.[28] They desired to play at governing. They lacked the wealth to amount to anything without control of the levers of political power. This they would share with Robles and company, but in 1934 and 1935, they were unwilling to permit the ultras to plunge Spain into the uncertainties of the totalitarian state. Furthermore, despite the bloodbath of Asturias, the mood of the country remained revolutionary, with the untapped strength of the millions that Caballero's playing with insurrection had left unmobilized, hence alive, angry and desperate.[29]

If the Left had failed in its revolutionary effort to preserve the Republic from its sworn enemies, the Right made a counter-revolution that was incomplete, inefficient, pyrrhic.[30] The resistance of Asturias won time for the idea of a People's Front to take root in Spain. The center parties of the Republic began to coalesce and seek allies on the Left; proletarian unity was forged in the prisons and radiated outward from those centers of torment to embrace the whole peninsula.[31]

IV. *Finally, Frente Popular*

Thus, in the summer of 1935, the journey of Spanish Communist Party representatives, headed by La Pasionaria, to the VII Congress of the Comintern was not a pilgrimage to receive the word from Moscovy's dialecticians. It was, in fact, to place before the troubled shrine of Lenin's followers the lessons of Spanish experience: that only the broadest coalition of working class parties and *all other* political groups threatened by the rising tide of fascist barbarism could preserve a political base for future proletarian redemption.[32]

That this policy in Spain and France coincided with the military-political necessities of the USSR was mere incident. For all but a minority of Spaniards it was a question of movement into the twentieth century or a return to the night of medieval obscurantism made infinitely horrible by modern techniques of inflicting everlasting pain and humiliation.

The decision to call for elections on the part of the President, Alcalá-Zamora, was precipitated by sordid financial and moral scandals which discredited the old style politicians. Misreading the mood of the country, the President assumed that a Right-Center coalition would emerge which would be strong enough to maintain a constitutional lid on the revolutionary masses. The Right, remembering its triumph of 1933, achieved a semblance of unity for the electoral contest, but failed to develop a program for the country which could solidify all the conservative factions

19

in a concerted attack against what was thought to be a defeated subversive enemy. The always amorphous Center shied away from the vindictive plans of Gil Robles and the other reactionary factions. Thus the Frente Popular pact, joining the Socialist and Communist Parties with the Center (Azaña, Martínez Barrio, the Catalan Esquerra and a portion of Basque Nationalists) united the working class parties with those of the small but influential liberal bourgeosie around a program which was essentially nothing more than a return to the promised social reforms of the first Republican Cortes.

Though marred by some frauds and scattered acts of violence and intimidation, the elections were reasonably honest. To the astonishment of the wealthy reactionaries of town and country who had spent their millions in a vicious campaign against Republicans of all shades, the Frente Popular won. The victory was not overwhelming in terms of popular votes: Left—4,700,000; Right—4,000,000; Center—449,000. But the electoral law which had favored the Right in 1933 now worked to the advantage of the stronger coalition of the Left. The Frente Popular received 257 of the 453 seats in the Cortes; the Right, 139; the Center, 57. Twenty seats were to be determined in a run-off election.

To a large extent, the Frente Popular victory was due to the precarious unity of the working class parties, above all to the participation of the apolitical anarchists who voted to free their comrades from prison.[33]

The reaction throughout the country was an exaggerated repetition of the enthusiasm which had greeted the fall of the monarchy in 1931. The prison gates were thrown open without awaiting official sanction or amnesty from the central government.[34] The embittered victims of 1934 raised the political temperature of the victors, who tended to forget that the electoral pact promised bourgeois reform, not a revolutionary reconstruction of Spain according to socialist

or libertarian blueprints. Although an honorable minority
of the Right proclaimed its acceptance of the verdict at the
polls, a powerful faction of ultra conservatives, monarchists,
military caudillos and outright fascists reacted to the February elections by accelerating the long deferred plans for a
military putsch.

In accordance with the pre-election agreements, state
power passed into the hands of the Republicans, with the
proletarian parties, led by the Socialists, playing the role
of a turbulent but loyal opposition on the Left, while the
conspiratorial Right began undermining the regime by
economic sabotage, verbal assaults of increasing virulence,
and almost open preparation for rebellion.[35] The Government, constituted by Azaña and his trusted friends, was
deceived by the peaceful transfer of power. Military figures,
including the conqueror of Asturias, General Franco, had
offered the army in support of a dictatorship and the annull-
ment of the elections. Azaña, trusting to his intuition, and
ignoring warnings of a well-knit plot, preferred to tem-
porize, fearing that any repressive action against the conspirators might trigger an uncontrollable response by the
furious masses of town and country.[36] Thus, while strikes
of increasing bitterness disrupted the cities, and tens of
thousands of peasants, believing that the promised land
reforms were at hand, stormed the estates of the monarchist
grandees, the Government in Madrid remained paralyzed,
the prisoner of its fears and illusions. The violence of words
and manifestoes now expressed itself in assassinations and
burning churches. The Cortes, divided by patterns of hate
rather than by differences of programs for social reconstruction and reconciliation, could neither strengthen the executive nor pacify the country.

Meanwhile, as the military Junta, headed by Generals
Mola, Goded, Cabanellas and their associates in the Union
Militar Española, tidied up their plans, the majority of the
great families of Spain, following the well established pat-

terns of the menaced nobility of the eighteenth and nineteenth centuries, transferred their funds to foreign banks,
and then from comfortable exile, spread fantastic tales of
Spanish communism in the drawing rooms of London, Paris
and Washington. Representatives of the putschists parlayed
with the Nazi hierarchy in Berlin, with representatives of
the Italian air force in Rome, and with leading personalities
of the diplomatic corps in Paris—still shaken by the German
reoccupation of the Rhineland on March 7.[37]

In June the Madrid Government, jolted from its lethargy
by alarming reports of loyal army officers, began to shift
suspected rebels from strategic commands, sending Franco
to the Canary Islands, Goded to the Balearics. This, too,
was an act of self-deception as it ignored the existence of
the airplane and the short wave radio. Furthermore, Azaña's
friends committed the inexcusable blunder of leaving the
arch conspirator General Mola in command of the Pamplona garrison, in the very center of the retrograde Carlist
peasantry, the one solid mass of civilian supporters of the
plotters. A series of political murders, culminating in the
assassination of the right wing Caudillo, Calvo Sotelo, on
July 12, forced the hand of the plotters. Pressured by the
civilian Falange, the rebel headquarters in Lisbon signaled
for the revolt to begin at dawn, July 17, in the Spanish
African garrisons.

V. *Rebellion and Revolution*

The Junta of the rebel generals who rose against the Republic in the summer of 1936 did not anticipate more than a mopping up operation of a few weeks. Aware of the weakness and vacillation of the Government, contemptuous of the masses of Spain whom they regarded as slave stock, essentially apolitical, thus ignorant of the fundamental social problems of Spain, they contemplated overwhelming pockets of resistance and establishing a military dictatorship. Recognizing that the Spanish military establishment was numerically insufficient to rule directly a hostile population, they planned from the beginning to ensure compliance by terror and through the premeditated extermination of all potentially hostile political groupings, to conduct themselves throughout the entire country in the manner of the Asturian pacification operation.[38]

General Queipo de Llano, the son-in-law of ex-President Alcalá-Zamora, exaggerated only slightly when he boasted in the first days of the war, "Mola, Franco and Cabanallas agree with me that it is a stupidity to want to save the lives of three or four hundred thousand persons, because if that number dies in Madrid, all will be over. Our plans have been worked out in accord with Germany and Italy. The Spaniards who will have to die for our final triumph approximate to three or four millions, and if these do not die fighting on the battle-fields, upon my honor, they will die shot or mutilated by our Legionnaires or Moors. If we do not do this, we should fail to carry out the promise we made to our brothers, the Germans and Italians. And we are all men of honor." [39]

The errors of the Government in Madrid, its complacency in the face of the planning of the rebellion, were now compounded as the ministers read the frantic telegrams from loyal supporters in the colonies and the provincial capitals. Instead of summoning the population to arms, instead of responding to the desperate warnings of the working class parties and trade unions, the ministers attempted to parley with the traitorous officers and issued pathetically mendacious bulletins concerning the calm in the country. The results were calamitous. Provincial officials and security forces not committed irrevocably to the putsch now went over to the rebellion. The population outside of the largest cities was kept in ignorance of the course of events and hence was unable to mobilize for self-defense. [42]

Thus were lost in the first days not only the overseas possessions—above all, Morocco, with the largest and most effective military establishments—but the important proletarian bastions of Saragossa in Aragon and Oviedo in Asturias were overwhelmed, as were the southern gates to Spain: Sevilla and Cadiz. Pamplona, Burgos, Salamanca, Valladolid, Ávila, Córdoba, Huelva, Granada were seized by the soldiers with the connivance of treacherous civilian officials.

Where the working class parties were well organized— above all, in Madrid, Barcelona, Valencia and Bilbao—the uprising of the army was met by successful revolution, and the tottering Republic was saved by the spontaneous heroism of the civilians, ably seconded by handfuls of loyal soldiers and officers. Thus, the great cities of Spain, the cradle of the Republican movement, were held by the initiative of the people who paid for the victory by piling high their mountains of corpses. The mining and metallurgical centers of the north and central regions with most of the industry; the ports of Gijón, Málaga and Cartagena, with half the navy; most of the small air force, with a score of old planes —such was the balance of the rebellion forty-eight hours after General Franco had been flown from the Canary Islands to Morocco in a Lufthansa plane, piloted by associates of the British Intelligence Service. Rallied to the rebel cause were the wheat and cattle producing areas of old Castile, with large but staunchly Republican areas, overpowered by the military garrisons. From the point of view of human and natural wealth, the people had salvaged the major resources of Spain. The element of surprise had won for fascism at best a precarious foothold.[41]

From the smoke and carnage in Madrid, Barcelona, Valencia and Asturias, there arose a new power in Spain: the people in arms—arms given reluctantly by timid politicians or seized from defeated regiments of the rebellion. A new Government, headed by Republican Prime Minister José Giral, but supported by working class parties and unions, took up the challenge of domestic counter-revolution and its foreign supporters.

Had Spain in the third week of July, 1936, been isolated from the world, the putsch would have been crushed. The rebels, however, were saved by the intervention of Germany, Italy and Portugal and the cowardly response of England, France and the United States.

VI. *Intervention and Non-Intervention—First Phase*

With their plans for a quick coup shipwrecked by the fury of popular resistance, with militia columns formed by the political and trade union leaders pouring out of the big cities to secure the countryside and penning up General Mola's forces in the mountains, the rebel generals were staring at certain defeat. Their main body of armed men was in Spanish Morocco, separated by nearly 1,000 miles of hostile Spain from the old Carlist redoubts. Furthermore, the loyal Republican navy was steaming southward to block exit from the African ports.

At this juncture Hitler, Mussolini and Salazar, the clerical-fascist Portuguese dictator, saved the fascist cause. The Germans sent thirty Junker-52 transports to Africa, which flew over France on July 18. Another group of Italian transport planes, which had been alerted by Mussolini on July 15, joined in the operation. By August 15, in the first great strategic airlift in history, the Army of Africa, twenty thousand battle-hardened troops, the Spanish Foreign Legion, and Moroccan mercenaries secured a *place d'armes* in Sevilla and Cadiz where, amply supplied with modern German planes and tanks, they streamed northward towards Madrid.[42] Oil for this operation was supplied by American companies, delivered on credit to the rebel generals against promissory notes which could only be cashed when the gold and silver reserves then totally controlled by the Republic were in the hands of the rebels. Meanwhile Spanish Republican warships, charged with the mission of holding

26

the sea lanes to the Spanish mainland, were refused petroleum supplies when they put into Gibraltar.[43]

Faced with this crisis of legitimate self-defense, the Spanish Prime Minister José Giral directed an agonizing appeal to the newly installed Popular Front Government of France headed by M. Leon Blum. The French Government was bound by solemn treaty obligation to supply the arms requirements of the Spanish Republic. Leon Blum was linked by ideological as well as strategic ties to Spain. He had been swept into office by the same social forces that sustained the Frente Popular of Spain. It was the fear of domestic and foreign fascism that had made this socialist, this humanist, this Jew, Prime Minister of France. Four days before the rebellion of the Spanish generals, Bastille Day celebrations in Paris had turned into the greatest popular demonstration against fascism since the rise of Hitler. Furthermore, the French Government was fully aware of the intervention of the German and Italian air forces on the side of the rebels. Nonetheless, Blum refused the arms which might have made the Pyrenees frontier a bastion of popular democracy. The socialist Prime Minister yielded to two threats: the French quasi-fascist Right through its control of the major newspapers portrayed Spain as wallowing in torrents of Bolshevik-shed blood, and warned of a similar civil war in France if the Jew Blum gave arms to be used against the future rulers of Spain. These fantasies of the French Right were paralleled by a more deadly menace from the British Conservative Government. It was made unmistakeably clear to the French Prime Minister that should France become involved in a wider war developing from the Spanish conflict, France could not rely upon the support of Britain. Thus, under pressure from the French bourgeoisie, whipped into white-hot anger by the "New Deal" type reforms which terrified the French and English industrial classes, the French Government initiated the series of diplomatic moves which led swiftly to the formation of the London Committee of Non-Intervention.[44] Thus was born the policy, to which the Soviet Union at first adhered and which was later to be reinforced by an American arms embargo, which resulted in the boycott of the legally constituted government of Spain in the months when the totalitarian powers began to pour arms into the rebel-held ports and prepared for the eventual dispatch of entire expeditionary corps.[45]

As the Army of Africa, four miniature mechanized divisions headed north towards Madrid, the deportment of Britain's oldest ally, Portugal, became decisive. Here in Lisbon and Estoril the rebels had planned the rebellion. From the earliest days, German supplies were unloaded in Portuguese ports; rebel ships en route from Africa to the northern fronts refueled in Lisbon; loans for the rebels were floated by Portuguese banks; Portuguese munitions plants worked day and night for the rebels; Portuguese air bases were used by German bombers that opened the way north for Franco's mercenaries; communications between Franco and Mola were maintained by the telegraph and telephone networks of Portugal. Spanish civilians, fleeing from the path of the Moors across the border, were turned over to the Falange and shot.[46]

Although the tortuous diplomacy which summoned into being the macabre farce of the London Non-Intervention Committee was French in execution, the design was British and reflected that same warped vision of European realities destined to reach its bloody climax on the beaches of Dunkirk. Though great armies would march and counter-march and tear each other to shreds in Spain, the demigods in London always held the threads of their fate, and from the beginning, tipped the scales toward a fascist triumph. In late July and early August German and British warships had prevented the Republic from bottling up the main rebel force in Africa. British connivance was not lacking in the fateful treachery of the Portuguese. What had already happened to deliver Ethiopia to Mussolini's Blackshirts was merely continued in Spain. The vacillating French, unwilling accomplices in Africa, paralyzed in the Rhineland, in yielding to British pressure and bluff, in answering the appeal of the Spanish Republic with a tearful "No," took a long step towards Munich and the shame of Vichy.[47]

Because essentially the fate of Spain was to be decided in London, despite the belated intervention of the Soviet Union on behalf of the Republic, it is the attitude of the enlightened conservatives, above all of Winston Churchill and his supporters, that must be examined. Writing at a time when the Spanish monarchists were conspiring with domestic and foreign fascists for the destruction of the Republic, Winston Spencer Churchill found nothing but praise for King Alfonso XIII and nothing but contempt for the Republican forces whose revulsion against the ancient crimes of the monarchy had driven the last of the Bourbons into exile. With a vast private intelligence service at his disposal, Churchill saw the Spanish disaster as evidence of a communist plot which had plunged Spain into the "present hideous welter against the desires of the overwhelming majority of Spaniards on both sides." Sympathy for the exiled Spanish dukes was understandable, but the repetition of every slander against the Spanish Republic by the most enlightened British statesman did much to hasten that accretion of German and Italian power which Churchill was pledged to prevent.

When Soviet aid began to be a major factor on the side of the Republic, the old organizer of the wars of intervention against the Soviet Union wrote: ". . . the dull squalid figures of the Russian Bolsheviks are not redeemed in interest even by the magnitude of their crimes. All form and emphasis is lost in a vast process of Asiatic liquifaction. Even the slaughter of millions and the misery of scores of millions will not attract future generations to their uncouth lineaments and outlandish names." And in another passage, showering praise on Boris Savinkov, the organizer of the pistol assault on Lenin, Churchill referred to his old enemies as "the cold Semitic internationalists," thus echoing the Nazi-style slogans being shouted by the Falangists in Burgos and Salamanca.[48]

These attitudes, typical of the Tory elite, were reinforced by the prospect that the vast holdings of the British investors in Spain, the important copper, iron and mercury mines, would be nationalized by a victorious worker-dominated Republic. Ignored was the equally obvious fact that a victorious rebel junta owing its triumph to German and Italian arms, would make these same resources available to the armament industries of the nascent Axis.

Thus, with German and Italian representatives sitting as honored members of the London Committee of Non-Intervention while German and Italian arms poured into the rebel arsenals of Spain, the half-armed Spanish militia vainly attempted to halt the thrust towards Madrid. In the flat plains of Andalusia the rebels' mechanized forces were irresistible.

"What was the technique of this phenomenal advance? The army would proceed in coaches looted from the villages, eighty of them packed with Legionnaires, forty of them with Moors, eight lorries of ammunition, a signal wagon, an ambulance, a petrol tank on wheels, a touring car with machine guns. On the roof was loot, on the radiators religious emblems. This is their procedure: they roll up the Madrid road over an elevation in the wide valley. They see a village, a cluster of houses with a church in great outlines above them. As they come in sight, a flash in the light morning air, and shells burst above them. The men jump from their coaches, hurry on with their machine guns. The wireless sends out a call for planes. Guns play across the road, along it. They cut down the militia as the barber cuts off thick hair . . . the men lie down on the road, only a twitch of the limb and a pool of blood to tell the others that the road is death; and they scatter in the fields. And by now the planes appear. Flying low, they bomb the fields, drive the men back to the road, as a barking dog rounds up sheep. But the planes are upon them with machine guns, and harry them until few are left." [49]

The Republican Government's agony on the battlefield was compounded by anarchy in the rear. The Giral government was powerless, lacking police forces and a popular base. For the first two months after the uprising a spontaneous Red terror corresponding to the September massacres of the Fernch Revolution sought out the open and hidden supporters of the rebellion and delivered them to firing squads.[50] By the end of September, but when the gates to Madrid lay open, Francisco Largo Caballero, supported by the majority of the working class factions, formed a government and began painfully and slowly to reconstitute the authority of the new Spanish State. In these circumstances, and under pressure from the French Communist Party, the Soviet Union drew back from the pledge to the London Non-Intervention Committee and began the dispatch of military advisers and modern military equipment to the Republic.[51] Early in October, with Madrid threatened by encirclement, the Soviets agreed to call into existence international brigades.[52]

The shift in Soviet foreign policy transformed the nature of the Spanish conflict. Having no direct stake in Spain, either of an economic or military nature, but being the ultimate sponsor of the policies of the Frente Popular and the Front Populaire of France, the Russian dilemma was acute. Moscow placed great importance on the Russo-French military pact. But the French Government (under British Conservative pressure) had espoused non-intervention on the grounds that the Spanish conflagration should be confined to the Iberian peninsula. However, should Spain become a base of German military power (so reasoned the Russian General Staff), the value of the French army as an ally of the Red army in a predictable clash with Nazi Germany would be greatly depreciated. If, as a result of a communist-socialist conflict over the Spanish issue, the Front Populaire should fall, the probabilities were that the pact between Moscow and Paris would become a mere scrap of paper. Thus, when the decision to support the Spanish Republic was made, it was coupled with a political offensive to support the Front Populaire. As the Comintern's Secretary General, Georgi Dimitroff, put it, "The situation may be reduced to the following: to exert every effort to help the Spanish people crush the fascist rebels; not to allow the People's Front in France to be discredited or disrupted; to hasten by every means the establishment of a World People's Front of struggle against fascism and war." [53]

Thus towards the end of September, 1936, there began to arrive in Spain Soviet military technicians of the first rank: Stern, Goriev, Berzin, Konev, Malinovsky, Zhukov, Chuikov, Voronov, Meretskov, Rodimstev—the future defenders of Moscow, Leningrad and Stalingrad and the conquerors of Berlin (May, 1945).[54] Their arrival followed by several months the appearance at rebel headquarters of many of Hitler's future World War II commanders: Generals of the Luftwaffe Jannecke and Sperrle, Admiral Canaris, General von Thoma of the future Afrika Korps, Heinz Guderian, future Panzer Commander in Poland, France and Flanders, General von Richtofen, and hundreds more of the future Wehrmacht elite, learning in Spanish fields the evolving tactics of *blitzkrieg* and *schrecklichkeit*. Grouped in the Condor Legion and constantly fed replacements and reinforcements from Germany, they turned the Army of Africa, with its tanks, 88 mm. guns and airplanes, into a formidable juggernaut.[55]

To Barcelona as Consul General came Antonov Ovseenko, commander of the Red Guards who had stormed the Winter Palace for Lenin's revolution in October, 1917. There also arrived the experts of the secret police and experienced veterans of a hundred Comintern enterprises.[56] Moscow remembered the lessons of the Russian civil war and tended to interpret Spanish events in the light of their own experience.[57] The political experts, wise enough to realize that geography would prohibit the Soviet Union from matching the resources of Germany, Italy and Portugal, worked from the first moment to confine the political passions of the Spanish Republican masses within a framework that would not irrevocably antagonize the ruling elites of England and France.[58] While Franco's columns butchered their way through Andalusia, the Spanish Communist Party, assisted by its foreign experts, called into being a miniature army of its own, the famous Fifth Regiment, and sent it in its thousands under amateur officers armed with pistols and shotguns to hold the roads to Toledo.[59] At the same time, elements of the Fifth Regiment and socialist, anarchist and republican militia columns blocked the mountain passes to the north and west that led to Madrid. In the Sierra Guadarrama, where Spaniard fought Spaniard and where there was no mechanized equipment, the militia held its own.[60] In the flat plains to the south where Africans advanced, armed by the best of European arsenals, the militia was helpless.

In mid-August the rebels stood before Badajoz, the fall of which would link Franco's armies with those of General Mola. The rebel historian, Robert Sencourt, described this action in the following manner:

"For twenty-four hours, the desperate fighting continued. As soon as the guns had made a sufficiently large opening, the troops rushed upon them from San Cristóbal, while the legionnaires of the Sixteenth Company, advancing direct from Mérida, attacked the Trinity Gate. . . . The trumpet sounded for the attack, and drawing their knives, the men in the élan of the lust of battle sharpened by the vibrant note of drum and bugle, rushed toward the gate. They were met by the murderous swift shooting of machineguns, and driven back: but the Foreign Legion, with that desperate valour for which it was famous, advanced a second time. On their lips was the song which proclaimed that their chosen bride was Death. Out of a detachment of 180, eighty of them fell, including all their officers. But those who survived rushed on undeterred over the writhing bodies of their comrades to assail the actual operatives of the guns, whom they dispatched with bayonet and dagger. . . . In the streets, men still fought, from the center of the city to the outlying quarters. . . . But no militia, no guerrilleros could maintain themselves against the training, the discipline and the science of the troops from Africa. . . . There were stories of executions so ruthless that they sent a thrill of horror through the world. If was said that the invading troops shot two of the militia on the very steps of the high altar of the cathedral. It was said that 1,200 or even 2,000 of the militia were massacred. . . ." [61]

Close to 3,000 of the defenders of Badajoz were butchered in cold blood in the bull ring of the town. The act was profoundly symbolic. Spain had been transformed into the bull ring of the world, and though all the world was at first but spectator, three years later it would become participant. Like the bombing of Guernica, the holy city of the Basques, by German planes a year later, the crime of Badajoz profoundly shocked world public opinion.[62] The issues raised by the Spanish conflict ceased to be the domestic concern of Spaniards alone; and Spain, where nothing much had happened for centuries, became the second homeland of the generation which had emerged since the end of the First World War. But although American Senators denounced the fascist crimes, though anguished questions were hurled at prime ministers in the sedate House of Commons, the grim farce of the Non-Intervention Committee continued, and Franco's armies marched successfully to the relief of Toledo, and on September 28, stood within seventy kilometers of Madrid.

While the Republic was still struggling to establish its

authority throughout the areas loyal to it, General Francisco Franco, Supreme Commander of the fascist forces of land, sea and air, was also made rebel Chief of State, and thus a single will, through the mechanism of an implacable military dictatorship, was able to mobilize the entire resources of the fascist cause and establish the political base for future military success.[63] There is irony in the agony that was Spain. General Franco had risen, he said, to save Spain from bolshevism, where none had existed, but he had been instrumental not only in bringing the Moorish army back to Spanish soil; he had also provided the occasion for a communist-led army to spring into being to oppose, under the banner of the hammer and sickle, those Islamic forces driven from Spain five centuries before.

In September, October and November the Bedouin, Arab, Berber and Riffian troops, moving from Córdoba through Toledo to El Escorial of Philip II, encountered first the Spanish battalions of the Fifth Regiment, bearing the exotic names *Thaelmann, Sailors of Kronstadt, Paris Commune, Leningrad,* and the more Hispanic but equally exotic titles of *Red Lions, October, Worker and Peasant Youth, Red Bullets, Iron Madrid Commune, Students' Federation, Asturias, Jaén, Lister, Campesino, Bácker, Feder, Legal, Primera Unidad de Avance,* and thirty-three separate companies that called themselves *Acero* (Steel).[64]

Against desperate but spasmodic resistance, the African Army cleared the approaches to Spain's capital. Equipment from the Soviet Union had been unloaded in Mediterranean ports, but the Government, dominated by Francisco Largo Caballero, Prime Minister and Minister of War, failed to establish an effective central command, failed to militarize transport, failed to build fortifications beyond artillery range of the capital's heart, failed to organize guerrilla bands, failed to purge the War Ministry of officers committed to the fascist cause. Debacle followed debacle, and in the first days of November the outward defenses of

Madrid collapsed. Rebel planes appeared unopposed in the skies dropping bombs and leaflets: "Inhabitants of Madrid, resistance is useless! Help our troops take the city. Otherwise the Nationalist aviation will wipe it from the earth. Militia and workers of Madrid: throw down your arms and free yourselves from the lying leaders who deceive you. We will know the guilty and only on them will fall the weight of the law. A single cry must unite us: Viva España! . . . General Franco."

The generals were in a hurry. Their operational plans had called for the occupation of Madrid on October 12 to celebrate Columbus Day. Early in the month Madrileños had scoffed at the rebel threats. Now with streams of refugees pouring in, and fascist bombers raining death, General Mola announced that the city would be stormed on the 7th of November to commemorate the Bolshevik Revolution. The right wing press and radio around the world echoed the imminent triumph of fascism.

VII. *The Battle for Madrid*

With the capital nearly ringed by hostile forces, the Government of Republican Spain departed for Valencia, trusting the defense of the city to General José Miaja and a Junta of Defense. Thus, while the rebel command paused outside the city, completing the detailed plan for what it thought to be one final thrust to victory, the population, freed from the incubus of pessimism and defeatism embodied in the governmental apparatus, prepared to defend itself. Under the stimulus of the working class parties and the youth organizations, barricades arose and elements of the Fifth Regiment general staff, assembling under huge posters and streamers which stated, "Madrid shall be the tomb of world fascism," began to organize the city's people into companies and battalions.

On the 5th of November the first Soviet fighter planes had appeared in Madrid skies, driving away German bombers. The battalions of Commander Enrique Lister of the Fifth Regiment, which was bearing the brunt of the defense, had heard of the phantom army of the international volunteers gathering south of the capital in Albacete. The rebels, aware of the flight of the government, were convinced that the battered remnants of oft-defeated militia bands whom they had pursued from Sevilla would dissolve when the Condor Legion batteries renewed their drum fire. The generals' conception of Spain was strangely similar to that of the defeatist intellectual, José Ortega y Gasset, who had said of his country, "Spain went on wasting away. Today

37

we are not so much a people as a cloud of dust that was
left hovering in the air when a great people went galloping
down the highroad of history."

But on the 7th of November when the great assault
began, the civilians of Madrid, behind mined bridges and
the barricades built by their children, awaited with such
guns and home-made bombs as the Junta of Defense, under
the able directorship of Lt. Colonel Vicente Rojo, had made
available to them. The attacking generals learned, in fact,
what Napoleon Bonaparte had discovered about Spain a
century and a quarter before when he, "like all his contemporaries, having considered Spain as an inanimate
corpse, was fatally surprised at the discovery that when the
Spanish state was dead, Spanish society was full of life,
and every part of it overflowing with powers of resistance." [65]

Madrid resisted. With its artillery batteries silenced, its
few tanks disabled, short of machine guns, battalions of
workers, mobilized by the Madrid radio, formed a living
wall. The Fifth Column, hearing the crescendo of fascist
guns, attempted to disorganize the city's defense. It was
exterminated.[66]

The lines bent, but they did not break. Moroccan van-
guards, driven by the inflexible wills of their commanders,
penetrated the city only to be wiped out in ferocious hand-
to-hand combat. At the supreme crisis of the battle when
casualties had reduced the defenders by two-thirds, an
apocalyptic appeal was broadcast over Madrid's radio:

> "People of Madrid! History has presented you in this
> hour with the great mission of rising up before the
> world as the obelisk of Liberty. You will know how to
> be worthy of so exalted a destiny. You will tell
> the world how men defend themselves; how people
> fight; how Liberty triumphs. You will tell the world

that only a people that knows how to die for Liberty can live in freedom.

"People of Spain! Put your eyes, your will, your fists at the service of Madrid. Accompany your brothers with faith, with courage, send your possessions, and if you have nothing else, offer us your prayers. Here in Madrid is the universal frontier that separates Liberty and Slavery. It is here in Madrid that two incompatible civilizations undertake their great struggle: love against hate; peace against war; the fraternity of Christ against the tyranny of the Church. . . .

"Citizens of Madrid! Each of us has here on this soil something that is ash; something that is soul. It cannot be! It shall not be that impious intruders trample the sacred tombs of our dead! The mercenaries shall not enter as heralds of dishonor into our homes! It cannot be! It shall not be that the somber birds of intolerance beat their black wings over the human conscience. It cannot be! It shall not be that the Fatherland, torn, broken, entreat like a beggar before the throne of the tyrant. It cannot be! It shall not be! Today we fight. Tomorrow, we conquer. And on the pages of history, Man will engrave an immense heart. That is Madrid. It fought for Spain, for Humanity, for Justice, and with the mantle of its blood sheltered all the men of the world. Madrid! Madrid!" [67]

On November 8th, as the rebel offensive was renewed, the Eleventh International Brigade marched through the streets of Madrid and deployed immediately in the most threatened sectors. Composed of battalions of Germans, French and Slavs, bearing the names *Edgar André, Commune de Paris,* and *Dombrowski,* less than three thousand

strong, bringing with them only standard infantry equipment, but steeled in a score of revolutions, they turned back
within the shadow of Madrid's skyscrapers the Army of
Africa which carried the hopes of a speedy fascist triumph.
Their example inspired the militia. Franco's armies, which
had conquered entire provinces with scanty losses, melted
away in the narrow streets and in the wreckage of Madrid's
once beautiful University City. Directed by a Red Army
general and attacking with fixed bayonets, the International
Brigades stabilized the Madrid front during the first two
weeks of November, 1936. Though they paid for their ex-
ploit with thirty percent dead, these Brigades, drawn from
all political faiths and from the four corners of the world,
began at Madrid the function of providing a living wall, behind which the Spanish Republican Government completed
the building of a people's army. So high were the losses of
the attacking fascist forces that the Junta of generals considered that the war was lost. Again they were to be rescued
by the diplomacy of the fascist powers and the cowardice
and stupidity of London and Paris. On November 23 the
governments of Italy and Germany conferred diplomatic
recognition upon the rebel Junta. General Franco responded
to this honor by reminding the world that Germany, Italy
and Portugal formed the bulwark of culture, civilization and
Christianity in Europe. He reiterated the fraudulent claim
that the generals' rebellion was undertaken to save Spain
from Russian Sovietism.[68] When questioned in the House of
Commons two days later, the Right Honorable Anthony
Eden denied that the recognition of a camarilla constituted
intervention in the affairs of Spain. The Non-Intervention
Committee was thus turned into a sinister shield for fascist
imperialism.

Reading the intentions of the Conservative Government
more clearly than either the British public or the supine
British Labor Party, the German and Italian dictators ac-

celerated and expanded their intervention in the Spanish conflict. The Condor Legion was strengthened. Four divisions of the Italian army, together with vast quantities of military supplies, were readied for dispatch to Spain. The terrible gaps torn in Franco's mercenary Moroccan forces were filled by recruiting carried out in French Africa by wealthy members of the French Right.[69] Supporters of the Spanish Republic, aroused by the sacrifices of the International Brigades, raised more volunteers, protested against embargoes and neutrality acts. Not until warfare blew with iron wind through the jungles of southeast Asia would an issue of foreign policy ever again so deeply touch the hearts and minds of ordinary men and women. But the appeals to conscience, to national interest, or to the vanishing sense of human solidarity, were to fail.[70] No government, having once turned its back on the Spanish people, was ever to read the handwriting on the wall. They all watched while German bombers at the dawn of 1937 lit great fires in the heart of the Spanish capital. Occasionally there were protests about the inhumanity of attacking open cities, but no state save the Soviet Union sent anti-aircraft guns or fighter planes to beleaguered Madrid. Warsaw, Rotterdam, Coventry and a hundred more ancient cathedral towns would be bombed by the same pilots that tried to open the way for Franco's Moors to storm Madrid. But Europe's elites took what comfort they could from the hope that a war-ravaged Spain would be forced to look eventually to England and France for reconstruction capital—a mortgage banker's view of the world which, though sound enough, encouraged the alliance of Germany and Italy, forged in Spain, to grow strong enough to put London to the torch and make of France a conquered satellite.

For five months after the failure of the rebel storming operations at Madrid, the Spanish Republican capital remained the strategic goal of the fascist armies. Reinforced to 65,000 effectives, these forces launched successive encircling operations against the beleaguered city. Small towns now figured in the dispatches: Pozuelo, Húmera, Las Rozas, Majadahonde, Boadilla del Monte, El Escorial, then the Jarama Valley, and finally, Guadalajara. The pattern of these ferocious encounters repeated on a greater scale the savage November fighting in the suburbs of Madrid. German staff officers synchronized air attacks with the thrust of armored columns and mechanized infantry, perfecting the style of operations that in five years' time would put all of Europe under the Nazi boot. The Republican commanders replied with a fraction of the mechanized modern equipment arriving from the Soviet Union and made good the deficit with the bodies of the Republican militia and the corpses of the International battalions.[71] In this cauldron Republican Spain's young officers learned their trade, while their errors were reflected in the terrible casualty figures which sometimes reached fifty percent of the front-line troops. Checked in the mountain towns which ring Madrid, the rebel high command in the first week of February, 1937, sought to cut the lone highway linking Madrid with the Mediterranean seaports. In the Jarama Valley, through which the lifeline passed, crack Moroccan infantry, the Foreign Legion, German artillery units and Condor air squadrons were stopped by the immense sacrifices of four International Brigades and the Fifth Regiment's forces. Here for the first time fought the new American battalion, the Abraham Lincoln, which, on its first day of combat operations, left one-third of its effectives scattered through the olive grooves.[72]

The bloody stalemate in the Jarama Valley placed General Franco's forces in a familiar dilemma. His own resources were obviously insufficient to the task of breaking the will to resist of the popular masses mobilized under the Republican flag. Unlimited quantities of materièl could blunt any dangerous offensive of the emergent Republican army. His desperate need was for troops. These were now supplied by an honored participant in the deliberations of the London Committee of Non-Intervention. Early in February the vanguard of four regular Italian army divisions began to arrive in Spain. On February 9th the invaders won a cheap victory by conquering the ill-defended seaport town of Málaga. In the first week of March Benito Mussolini, scornful of the popular forces which had defended Madrid, decided that the glory of capturing the city belonged by ideological right to Fascist Italy. His 50,000 superbly equipped troops now formed the vanguard of the army which on March 8 undertook to thrust through Guadalajara and storm the city of Madrid.

The prelude to the battle was a communiqué from the fascist Grand Council which boasted of the victory soon to be achieved against bolshevism in the West. Mussolini, then playing the part of a Roman emperor in his visit to the Italian colony of Libya, was fully aware that the myth of fascist invincibility was now at stake, and he informed his legionnaires that the forces they faced were ideologically similar to those which his Fascisti bands had "thrashed in the streets of Italy." The weight of metal and the mass of armor broke the front, and the Black Flame and Black Arrow divisions rolled proudly towards beleaguered Madrid. But then was repeated the epic of November, 1936. The weary decimated units of the International Brigades and the Fifth Regiment were rushed in trucks from the Jarama Valley; eighty Russian airplanes rose in a protective umbrella; [73] anti-fascist volunteers of the Garibaldi Battalion spearheaded the Republican counter-attack. On the rugged storm-lashed plateau of Castile the Fascist army was routed, suffering approximately 12,000 casualties. With the nature of the conflict exposed for all the world to see, what was known as the Battle of Guadalajara could have been a turning point not only in the Spanish struggle, but in world history. Herbert Matthews of the New York *Times* reflected this feeling when he cabled the following:

> "None of us knew the full significance of what had happened, for we could not know that the Italians had not only been driven from another town, but were routed. Above all, we could not know the decisive character of the defeat. That was the important thing —that the defeat was decisive, that the stream of history had been deflected into new channels, that a change had taken place, not only in the war, but in the world.

> "Considering the preliminaries and the completion of the action afterwards, the battle of Brihuega [near Guadalajara] lasted fifteen days. I felt at the time, and now that fifteen months have passed, I feel even more strongly, that it will rank as one of the twelve or fifteen decisive battles of history. In my opinion, nothing more important has happened in the world since the European war than the defeat of the Italians on the Guadalajara front. What Bailén was to Napoleonic imperialism, Brihuega was to Fascism, and it will be that whatever may be the outcome of the Civil War." [71]

The Republic's soldiers, viewing the wreckage of Mussolini's army, thought they had caught a glimpse of the future of Fascism, and knowing of the shining, wonderfully outfitted ranks of Nazi youth which paraded at Nurenberg, they foresaw the day when these, too, would lie broken in the mud and filth.[75] They coined brave slogans after Guadalajara. They thought of Spain as the tomb of world fascism. They said that "the armies marching on Madrid, Barcelona and Valencia are also marching against London, Paris and Washington." This was true. But the politicians of the Western capitals, enmeshed in their petty diplomatic games and lacking a world vision, preferred the victory of Franco and his foreign allies to a triumph of the popular forces backed by Moscow, which would have fatally undermined the German and Italian regimes and placed on the agenda of the day the agonizing problem of where the frontiers of socialism should be drawn.

VIII. *The War—Second Phase*

After the fascist rout at Guadalajara, Madrid ceased to be the primary target of Franco's armies. Reinforced by Italian divisions and secure in the pledge of unlimited German equipment, the center of gravity of the war was shifted to the northern provinces—the Basque country and Asturias. Republican access to these areas had been cut off in September of 1936 when the defenders of the northern gateway to Spain, Irún, were overwhelmed while trainloads of munitions were stopped just beyond the International Bridge by Premier Blum's non-intervention policy. The fate of the main bastion of Republican power, the great industrial city of Bilbao, was sealed when the British government recognized the illegal blockade of the Basque ports.[76]

Proud in their autonomy, the middle class leaders of the Basque territory conducted a private war of resistance of their own. They refused to purge the Fifth Columnists and defeatists in their ranks who had intimate ties not only with Germany and Austria, but also with British banking and industrial circles. They built the famous iron belt in their mountains protecting the approaches to the city, but the secret of its construction was betrayed by a Basque official to the besieging armies. At the request of the Republican Government, a Russian mission headed by General Goviev, the organizer of Madrid's defense, went to Bilbao. A squadron of Russian planes arrived. Enrique Castro Delgado, one of the political movers of Madrid's mobilization, attempted to repeat the miracle of November 6 in Bilbao. He was poisoned. The large central armies around Madrid, exhausted by six months of uninterrupted fighting, were unable to mount offensives in time to pull the fascist reserves away from the beleaguered north. Refusing to fight in the streets of their city in the manner of the Madrileños, hammered by the reinforced Italian expeditionary corps, Bilbao fell on June 19, 1937. Thus the greatest industrial resources of Spain were delivered intact to the rebellion.[77]

The Republican Government, weakened by a Trotskyist-anarchist putsch in Barcelona in May,[78] horrified by the destruction of the port of Almería by the German pocket battleship *Deutschland*,[79] was reorganized under the leadership of the socialist Juan Negrín. Despite its reverses, the Republic, morale intact and still linked by the anti-fascist *mystique* created at Madrid to all the world, went on training its peasant recruits and amateur staff officers. During the first week of July, 1937, it fielded a regular army grouped in corps, divisions and brigades, and flung it against the forces laying siege to Madrid. Spearheaded by the five International Brigades, assembled for the first and last time near Madrid, the Republican Army fought a nightmarish campaign in the Sierra Guadarrama. Against crushing artillery, tank and air force odds, the Republican infantry fought to a bloody stalemate. The strategic initiative remained with Franco. The International battalions, which melted away in what was called the Battle of Brunete, had completed their mission.[80] The compact Spanish units which deployed in this campaign had emerged in nine months from the wreckage of the civilian columns which had been driven back to Madrid in November of 1936.

All that courage and the spontaneity of the people could accomplish had been achieved. The outcome of the war was now a cold question of logistics, a balancing of planes, guns, tanks and shells. The great arsenal of the Ruhr, the factories of Italy, the diplomacy of Great Britain—all of this sustained the fascist cause. The Republic's lifeline ran through a hostile Mediterranean rendered doubly perilous by Italian "pirate" submarines, to the depots of the Soviet army.[81] This power, threatened also by Japan in the east, had turned to support the hard-pressed armies of China. Joseph Stalin, self-trapped in the great purge trials of 1936-38, was forced to weigh the ideas of anti-fascist solidarity and collective security against the realities of non-intervention as practiced by the Western world. Fleets of armament-laden Russian trucks continued to roll uninterruptedly from Barcelona and Valencia to the insatiable fronts. A safe route ran from the Baltic to Bordeaux, and thence across the Pyrenees to Catalonia, but this route, which might have saved the honor as well as the political cohesion of the French people, was denied to Spain by the decaying French regime. The Republican Government of Spain, which had staked much upon a change of attitude in London and Paris, soon had to cope not only with the impoverishment of arms, but hunger, disillusionment, and political disunity in its civilian rear guard.[82]

In an effort to relieve the pressure on the isolated Asturian front, the Republic gathered its tired Madrid divisions and transferred them to the long dormant Aragon front. There, since the first days of the rebellion when the enthusiasm and guts of the anarchist worker militia had crushed the fascists, a ragtail army virtually independent of the central military staff had conducted a desultory war of its own. The walled cities of Jaca, Huesca and Saragossa, lightly garrisoned by the rebels, but well supplied with artillery and protected by powerful contingents of German and Italian airplanes, had invariably scattered the attacking columns.[83] On August 24, in a desperate effort to gain the strategic initiative, the Republican units tried to unhinge the area by storming the fortified towns of Belchite and Quinto. Weeks of bitter house-to-house fighting led to the capture of these redoubts with considerable loss of precious shock troops and equally irreplaceable armament, but the highly mobile forces of Franco sealed the breach in their lines without interrupting their strategic operations. The province of Asturias went down fighting, and Franco's Moors, remembering the bloodbath of 1934 and their terrible losses at Madrid, wreaked a grisly revenge on the defenseless miners.[84]

After the indecisive fighting in Aragon and with uninterrupted reinforcements of men and materièl assured by Germany and Italy, General Franco began a redeployment of his forces for a renewal of the long delayed storming of Madrid. The Republican Government, aware that the loss of the north posed a mortal threat to its survival, decided upon a desperate expedient. It swiftly gathered all of the armament available in Spain for an assault against the city of Teruel. It gambled that only an offensive success would restore the morale of the rear guard and convince world public opinion that all was not yet lost in Spain. On December 15, 1937, covered by a blinding snowstorm, they struck. With their planes grounded, with icy roads nearly impassable, the infantry divisions surrounded the city, and with grenade and machine gun, stormed it. The fall of Teruel forced Franco to suspend operations on the Madrid front; but his professional army, now highly mobile, swiftly mounted a counter-offensive with crushing superiority. For six weeks the Republicans held their ground doggedly, but finally fell back to avoid entrapment.[85]

The operation proved that technically the People's Army had matured, that it could attack as well as defend. But the amateur soldiers of the Republic misinterpreted the real meaning of the battle of Teruel. They failed to recognize a terrible truth: modern wars are not won by courage; there are limits to what morale can accomplish; tactical success can lead to a strategic disaster. For what the German staff officers already knew was this: war is a continuous process and must be sustained by an uninterrupted flow of materièl. Although the human element may be decisive in defense of cities, as demonstrated at Madrid, guns, transport, *food and oil* are decisive in the end.[86] After Teruel, London and Paris had to make the fateful reply to the appeal of the Republic. The answer was "No."

IX. *The War—Last Phase*

On March 9, 1938, strengthened by reinforced Italian divisions, and with their strategic reserves in the line, General Franco's armies opened a general offensive along a 100-kilometer front in Aragon. Enjoying a six to one superiority on the ground and ten to one in the air, the fascist forces achieved a rupture in depth and forced the shattered Republican divisions into a costly retreat which was not halted until Franco's Moroccans, Italians and Navarese reached the Mediterranean sea and thus cut the Republic in two. Though they sustained terrible losses, the Republican divisions did not disintegrate. Franco had hoped to expand the Aragon offensive into a victorious drive that would engulf Catalonia and the Valencia districts; but despite sabotage at the highest echelon of the Republican General Staff, the brigades which had saved Madrid arrived in time to stabilize the front.[87]

The crisis in Aragon coincided with the German thrust against Austria. On the same March day that Hitler occupied Vienna, Mussolini's armies poured through the Aragon passes. Four years before, when Hitler's Nazis attempted an Austrian coup, the Italian army had been rushed to the Brenner Pass. Now the Axis, forged in Spain, brought death simultaneously to the Ebro and to the Danube. The Italians, almost exactly one year after their rout of Guadalajara, paid their debt to Germany by delivering their erstwhile Austrian ally to the mercies of Hitler, whose *quid pro quo* to Mussolini was the delivery of sufficient arms to Spain to ensure a crushing fascist superiority in planes, tanks, artillery and munitions; and Franco, the bogus Nationalist, mortgaged the mineral wealth of Spain to Hitler's armament industry.[88]

At the height of the Aragon and Austrian crises, the French General Staff, reading the handwriting on the walls of Europe, prodded the weak French government into an awareness of the coming encirclement of France. Spanish Prime Minister Negrín was summoned to Paris. For one agonizing moment it appeared that the suicidal policy of non-intervention might be ended. French army forces in the southern military zone were alerted; nervous telegrams were exchanged between Salamanca, Paris and Berlin. But the rot in France had penetrated too deeply. The future heroes of Munich prevailed, and after a trickle of arms crossed the Pyrenees to Spanish Republican forces, the *diktat* of London was decisive. By mid-June of 1938 the French frontier was again sealed.[89]

Franco's backers were dismayed by the continuation of the Spanish conflict—with the dangerous display under the eyes of the entire world of what a people in arms could accomplish. London especially was infuriated by the anti-fascist temper that might prove contagious and that threatened the plans of Prime Minister Chamberlain to reach ever more wide-ranging accommodation with the Axis dictators.[90]

Had the Spanish Republican soldiers been motivated only by a sense of personal survival, as their national enemies hoped, or held in line by the machine guns of the commissars, as their foreign foes proclaimed, the army which was unhinged in Aragon could never have been reconstituted. But the reality was that the so-called "Reds" had the truly Catholic, that is to say, universal, view of the conflict. It was they who resisted the selling of Spain to the hated foreigner. They were the ones who voluntarily had formed themselves into an army and fought not only traditional oppressors, but alien conquerors, and did so with a clear understanding that the issue of the war transcended the local fate of their Republic.

The Republican Forty-Third Division, trapped in the foothills of the Pyrenees, held up the enemy for two weeks until food and bullets were exhausted. Then 4,000 strong retreated through waist-high snow to France. When French authorities offered the option of returning to battle in Catalonia or remaining in France, only 168 elected not to return to Spain's valleys of death.[91]

Angered by the high cost of continued Republican resistance, the fascist high command repeated its tactics of Madrid—*schrecklichkeit*—terror bombing—this time against Barcelona, now the seat of the Republican Government. Barcelona had suffered its first serious air raid on January 25. The attackers, Italian bombers based on Majorca, had the great port city at its mercy. The first raid killed several hundred civilians in the center of the city. Five days later the casualties reached 350. In mid-March the raids came every three hours, and in two days killed 1300 and injured 2000. These outrages stirred world opinion, but did not lead to the dispatch of fighter planes or anti-aircraft guns to Barcelona. The British government protested impartially to both sides. When embarrassing questions were raised in the House of Commons concerning this slaughter of the innocent. Mr. Neville Chamberlain said: "I do not believe that it would be difficult for the inhabitants to find refuge. I have read that there are numerous cellars in the vicinity." [92] A few weeks after the Barcelona terror raids, when Hitler had initiated the first phase of his offensive against Czechoslovakia, and when the Czech government was preparing to ship a substantial quantity of anti-aircraft guns to Spain, the Right Honorable Anthony Eden, Mr. Chamberlain's Foreign Secretary, interdicted the shipment.[93]

Despite the fact that the war had rolled up to the borders of Catalonia, the last industrial stronghold, the

Republic was far from defeated. Its armed forces numbered 600,000, and around Negrín were gathered political figures who were committed to a bitter-end struggle. Furthermore, the imminence of a German assault in middle Europe raised the prospect that in the event of a general war, the Spanish battlefields would be linked to a wider arena and thus receive the indispensable nourishment of supply that the starved divisions of the Teruel and Aragon fronts had so sorely lacked.

In mid-July the fascist offensive was renewed with the strategic objective of clearing the Mediterranean coast and conquering Valencia. The great port was protected on the land side by rugged terrain and excellent fortifications. Arms had arrived from the USSR and fresh troops were well SPAIN — GALLEY 19 placed. The Italians, believing that no Republican resistance was possible after their Aragon victories, attempted to storm the fortifications. The attack of 80,000 veteran Blackshirts was supported by 600 massed artillery pieces, by 400 bombers. Yet from the shell-torn trenches, the Republicans manned their machine guns despite a torrent of metal not seen in Europe since the worst land battles of the First World War. In eight days, the Italians suffered their worst massacre of the war—17,000 dead.[94] Then on July 25, the Republican Army, spearheaded by Colonel Juan Modesto's Fifth Army Corps, unleashed a surprise offensive, and in a feat of technical skill and incomparable elan, stormed across the Ebro River. Achieving tactical surprise and advancing with great gallantry without air or artillery cover, the Republic's assault drove the fascists in retreat, seizing thousands of prisoners and liberating scores of villages until, with supplies exhausted, the offensive halted and a grim four-month battle of attrition set in.[95]

While the guns on the Ebro roared the defiance of Republican Spain, the Czech crisis reached its climax. As antiaircraft guns were being mounted in Hyde Park, London, and in the parks of Paris, the Spanish fascists were shaken by panic. Guerrilla warfare, sabotage and assassinations were a grim reminder that the millions of Spaniards in Franco's territory were occupied, but not conquered.[96] Thousands of Franco's prisoners were rushed to build fortifications on the Pyrenees and in Spanish Morocco. The French discussed plans for the dispatch of their army to Catalonia.[97]

Then on the 30th day of September came Chamberlain's odious umbrella dance at Munich and the delivery of Czechoslovakia to Hitler. The night which descended on Prague deepened now in Barcelona and Madrid. With all hope of succor from the West abandoned, with high placed defeatists emboldened, the desperate Negrín government entered into secret negotiation with Generalissimo Franco— seeking an honorable settlement of the conflict. The answer from Franco was a cold and unyielding: no terms but unconditional surrender. Giving in again to the torturous diplomacy of London, Negrín agreed to the withdrawal of the International Brigades from the front. No longer could a few thousand volunteers tip the scales of the war, and the Spanish Republicans could only trust in the forlorn hope that the departure of the International Brigades would lead to effective world pressure to force the departure of Franco's German and Italian regulars. In a world in which the betrayal of the Czech ally was hailed as a feat of peace, the presence of foreign invaders on Spanish soil could no longer occasion any misgivings in the democracies.[98]

On November 15, as the last of the Republican forces withdrew in good order back across the Ebro River, 400,000 Spaniards bade farewell to the International Brigades as these paraded for the last time through the scarred and saddened streets of Barcelona. The farewell address for the Spanish Government was delivered by Dolores Ibarruri. In a city swarming with agents of the Fifth Column, swollen with refugees and the debris of the battlefields, she said:

"Comrades of the International Brigades: Political reasons, reasons of State, the welfare of that same cause for which you offered your blood with boundless generosity, are sending you back, some of you to your own countries and others to forced exile. You can go proudly. You are history. You are legend. You are the example of democracy's solidarity and universality, in face of the shameful, "accommodating" spirit of those who interpret democratic principles with their eyes on the hoards of wealth and industrial shares which they want to preserve from any risk. . . .

"When the olive tree of peace puts forth its leaves again, entwined with the laurels of the Spanish Republic's victory—come back!" [99]

On December 23, 1938, the curtain rose on the last major campaign of the Spanish conflict. The assault against Catalonia had begun. 350,000 troops, with a core of four completely mechanized Italian divisions, faced approximately 100,000 Republican soldiers, of whom less than half had adequate infantry equipment.[100] While the Ebro salient had been absorbing the main pressure of the fascist forces, the Republic had arranged for a formidable shipment of modern arms from the USSR: 250 airplanes, 250 tanks, 4,000 machine guns, 650 artillery pieces. This mass of equipment was loaded on seven Soviet ships in Murmansk and sent to French ports.[101] But the era of Munich had passed; the preparation for Vichy had begun. The Foreign Minister Bonnet prevented the delivery of the materièl which, if received in time, would have made the Catalan hills as dangerous for the attackers as the mountains in front of Valencia.[102]

Now was repeated on a vaster scale the retreat in Aragon. Unable to organize reserve units to plug the gaps ripped in their lines, the Republican armies were exposed in open terrain to the devastation of 600 bombers and raked by artillery massed one gun to every ten yards.[103] To the calamity of the armies was now added the panic of the cities and towns, hammered without mercy by fascist bombers. In pathetic and prophetic weeks, 500,000 civilians fled in terror along the choked storm-swept roads leading to the French frontier. The soldiers did what they could. Nuclei of resisters formed out of units which suffered up to eighty percent casualties, but the tide of misery was rolled irresistibly northward. On January 15, Tarragona fell; on January 26, a badly demoralized Barcelona was occupied without resistance. The Spanish Cortes, to the roar of expanding fascist bombs, met for the last time on February 1 in Figueras.[104] On February 4, the fronts dissolved, save for International volunteers who covered the retreat of the Spanish civilian refugees. The army, though forced back without reprieve, crossed the frontier in good order, most of its staffs intact, forced from the field, but unbroken.

Sixteen months later, a shattered and demoralized French army, assailed by the same enemy that had ravaged Spain, would be flung back toward these mountains—without honor, without the memories of the gallant Army of the Ebro whose long ordeal was now entered in the pages of history. Not with bugles and guards of honor were the Spanish soldiers received by the Latin sister, democratic France. Under the bayonetted rifles of Gardes Mobiles, Senegalese and Spahis, the rain-drenched battalions carrying their wounded and dying were herded off to improvised shelterless concentration camps hastily thrown up on waterless sand dunes. Surrounded by barbed wire—at Argelès, St. Cyprien, La Junquera—treated worse than prisoners of war, the wounded died first, then the children, then the old men and women. Dysentery, hunger and thirst—such was the finale to thirty-two months of anti-fascist struggle.[105] Such also was the moral level of France seven months be-

fore the German invasion of Poland would make World
War II official. On February 27, the British and French
governments extended diplomatic recognition to the rebel
Junta, thus crippling international action to succor the
refugees.

With the loss of Catalonia, the truncated Republic contained 9,000,000 half-starved souls, an army of perhaps
500,000, the fleet riding anchor impotently in Cartagena.
Victory was now but a tarnished dream clung to only by a
handful of Don Quixotes who saw in the menacing moves
of Hitler the certain flames of a world conflagration. Azaña,
Negrín, the generals and admirals knew that organized
resistance was hopeless; others, the commanders of the regiments that had survived the Catalonian holocaust, thought
of resistance as a means of forcing General Franco to moderate the terms of peace; they weighed the casualties of continued struggle against the numbers of defenseless men who
would be sent to the execution pits by the Falange's puni-
tive squads. They balanced death in the trenches against
death in prison courtyards. They remembered Badajoz and
Toledo and they preferred to die at their posts. They were,
however, largely communist by party affiliation. They were
an isolated minority.

British diplomacy in early March of 1939 helped weave
the strands of a new conspiracy against the dying Republic.
The powerful wireless of British warships, riding anchor
off the Spanish coast, established communications between
General Segismundo Casado and Julián Besteiro, leader of
the socialist defeatists, and Franco's headquarters.[106] On
March 5, 1939, after an unsuccessful coup in Cartagena,
the Casado Junta rose against Negrín. The Frente Popular
dissolved in a spasm of hate and fear. The units which had
held at Madrid for 1,000 days were set at each others'
throats. Proletarian brother butchered the ally of prouder
days while Franco waited—watching with bemused silence
while Casado's followers tried to prove that they were as

committed to the Holy Cause of anti-communism as the Falange.[107]

In the end it made no difference. The terms remained unconditional surrender. On Tuesday, March 28, 1939, at 11:00 a.m., the Italian troops entered Madrid by the Toledo Gate and the Moroccan cavalry paraded through the skeletal ruins of University City. Two days later, while thousands waited in the seaport towns for the evacuation ships which never came, the fascists completed the occupation of Spain.

The long fascist night began. It made of Spain a prison and a graveyard—an abode of silence, blood and tears where the generalissimo was Death.

Epilogue

During the Second World War, the Franco regime did all that was in its power to damage the cause of the United Nations.[108] Franco dispatched the Blue Division to fight with the Wehrmacht on the Eastern front. Falange agents helped to sabotage the defenses of Manila, while Franco's press hailed the American disasters in the Pacific. An army of Falange spies cooperated with Nazi submarines in the Caribbean and contributed massively to making those waters a graveyard of Allied ships. Warned personally by Admiral Canaris, a member of the German generals' conspiracy against Hitler, that the Axis would lose the war, Franco prudently refrained from declaring war, and thus escaped the fate of Hitler, Mussolini, Laval and Quisling.

Meanwhile, Spanish Republican exiles fought with the Free French in Africa, and by the thousands steeled the ranks of the French underground resistance army in southern France. Spanish Republicans rode the tanks of General Leclerc's army of liberation that drove the Nazis from Paris.

The bells which tolled for the anti-fascist victory in Europe on May 8, 1945, could be heard in the prisons of Spain. Twenty-one years later they still ring out, but the celebrants in Spain who contributed so much to that triumph are still prisoners, for though most of the steel and stone cages that for decades were the home of scores of thousands are nearly empty now, Spain is a prison for the spirit that created Don Quixote; that inspired the murdered poet, García Lorca; that sustained the art of Picasso and Casals.

Franco was created by the hot war of Hitler and Mussolini and preserved in power by the cold war of Churchill
and Truman. Spain is now an air base for the Americans,
as once it was for the fascists. The tourists come for the sun-
shine, the cheap peseta and the good wine. They drink and
dance where a generation ago a million men died. Far away
from the gaudy cities, in the mountains of Asturias and
Aragon, the peasants still place flowers on the graves of
the Republic's soldiers, for in their immemorial wisdom,
they know that Franco did not plant corpses, he planted
seed, and another generation awaits the harvest.

The Madrid Fronts October 1936 - March 1937

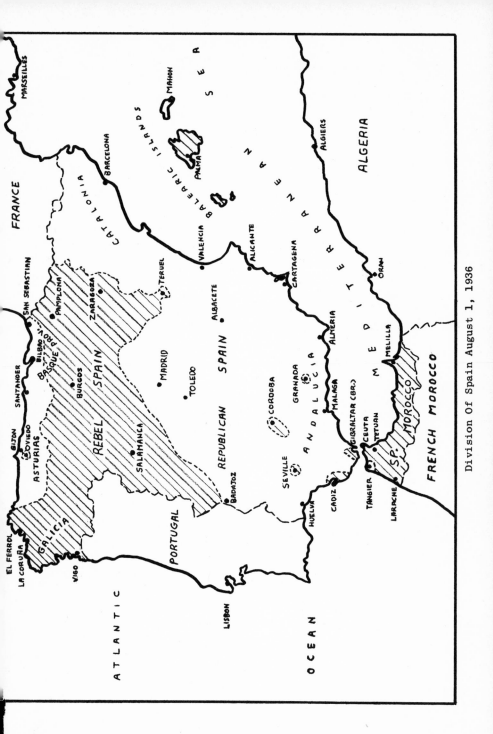

Division Of Spain August 1, 1936

NOTES

The object of these notes is not to indicate, let alone resolve, the conflicts of authorities, but to serve as a guide to the literature.

1. For the circumstances surrounding the fall of the monarchy, see Georges-Roux, *La Tragédie Espagnole* (Paris, 1963), pp. 12-19; Charles Foltz, Jr., *The Masquerade in Spain* (Boston, 1948), pp. 1-36. This, incidentally, is one of the most perceptive studies of modern Spain. It has been almost ignored by academic scholars. Another useful study of the fall of the monarchy will be found in A. Ramos Oliveira, *Politics, Economics and Men of Modern Spain, 1808-1946* (London, 1946), pp. 187-210.

2. A sympathetic analysis of a typical bourgeois republican, Manuel Azaña, is given by Frank Sedwick in *The Tragedy of Manuel Azaña and the Fate of the Spanish Republic* (Columbus, Ohio, 1963), *passim.* An unsympathetic but perceptive discussion of the Azaña type will be found in Salvador de Madariaga, *Spain* (New York, 1943), pp. 290-352.

   The agony of the Spanish middle classes, called too late in Spanish history, is set forth dramatically by Enrique Castro Delgado. He records the following conversation in a cafe with a friend of Azaña: "I do not think that Azaña knows either how to build a great Republic or what to do with one that he has. But he is the soul and brain of the Republic."

"No . . . he is a man upon whose tired shoulders the socialists without pity and without reason have unloaded the Republic. We are all Azaña, we of the middle class. We are a class which is very old. We have a great deal of dignity. We do not conduct strikes because we have everything that we need. We do not rise up in rebellion to preserve what we have. We feel it is our duty to keep the state machinery working. We are a class which has waited years and years in order to be able to speak, in order to be able to say what we believe must be done. Azaña speaks for us, but all he can do is speak. If he moves towards the Left, the Right will rise up. If he goes towards the Right, the Left rises."

"Then you believe Azaña is a fraud?"

"No. He is a frustrated man because he belongs to a frustrated social class. He knows that he has come too late. He knows that he is going to be sacrificed."— *Hombres Made in Moscu* (Mexico City, 1960), pp. 135-138.

3. For an analysis of the economic conditions of Spain, see Frank Jellinek, *The Civil War in Spain* (London, 1938), pp. 33-98; also Ramos Oliveira, *op. cit.*, pp. 211-262.

4. It is to be noted that the Spanish Republic had no diplomatic relations with the USSR; nor, until 1933, did the Comintern pay much attention to Spain. For a general profile of the oligarchy's mental and psychological state, see Foltz, *op. cit.*, *passim*. Interesting inside views of the Spanish aristocracy are provided by Ignacio Hidalgo de Cisneros, *Memorias*, Vols. I & II (Paris, 1964). Gabriel Jackson, *The Spanish Repub-*

lic and the Civil War, 1931-1939 (Princeton, 1965).
has an excellent summary of the ideological problems
of Spain in this epoch, particularly pp. 3-78.

5. For the social reforms of the first years of the Republic
    and the acute problems which these occasioned, see
    Ramos Oliveira, *op. cit.*, pp. 262-456. This author has
    made the most systematic sociological analysis of the
    Republic. The purely political issues relevant to this
    epoch are studied in depth by Carlos M. Rama, *La
    Crisis Española del Siglo XX* (Buenos Aires, 1960),
    pp. 13-193. Gabriel Jackson, *op. cit.*, deals insightfully
    with the same problems, pp. 56-98.

    A Falangist critique of Azaña's military reforms is
    contained in the volume by a leading conspirator
    against the Republic, General Emilio Mola, *El Pasado
    Azaña y El Porvenir* (Madrid, 1934). For a sober
    review of the ecclesiastical problem of the Republic,
    see the excellent study of José M. Sánchez, *Reform
    and Reaction, The Politico-Religious Background of
    the Spanish Civil War* (Chapel Hill, 1962), par-
    ticularly pp. 65-135.

    This issue, which was most clouded during and after
    the Spanish conflict, falls into better perspective when
    it is recalled that the clerical leaders attacked the
    Republic with unseemly verbal violence before any
    reform legislation was introduced in the Cortes. Many
    of the polemical writings about the church in Spain
    ignore the fact that by 1930 a great part of the tradi-
    tional wealth of the church was no longer in land,
    but in industrial shares and banking. With reference
    to this point, see Jellinek, *op. cit.*, pp. 33-98.

6. See Georges-Roux, *op. cit.*, pp. 32-34.

    The unemployment rate in Spain, only a partial
    index of urban misery, ran as follows during the first

years of the Republic: end of 1932—500,000; end of
1933—1,000,000; end of 1934—1,500,000.

7. For the problem of regionalism in Spain, see Rama,
   op. cit., pp. 13-33, 72-76; Jellinek, *op. cit.*, pp. 98-119;
   Ramos Oliveira, *op. cit.*, pp. 352-424; de Madariaga,
   op. cit., pp. 141-182.

8. The problem of the Spanish anarchists is the most
   complex and tragic in the history of modern Spain. A
   great deal that has been written about this movement
   misses the point. The critiques, be they liberal or
   Marxist, start from presuppositions which are totally
   rejected by Spanish anarchism. These concern the
   nature of man, the nature of society, and the meaning
   of liberty. The point is that the anarchists' credo is a
   world view which derives its inspiration from the pre-
   capitalist world and hence, to the anarchist the propo-
   sitions of Azaña, and generally those of Caballero,
   were not false; they were simply irrelevant. Jean
   Jacques Rousseau would have understood the Barcelona working class, but Lenin would have thrown up
   his hands in despair. Like the first industrial workers
   in Imperial Russia, many of the Spanish workers,
   recruited from the most backward agrarian parts of
   the country, brought into the factories and into the
   towns a psychology that was absolutely impervious
   to either capitalist or socialist-reformist appeals. It is
   highly probable that this same attitude is found today
   in many of the new cities of Asia, Africa and Latin
   America.

   Perhaps the most successful effort to understand
   anarchist political behavior is to be found in Gerald
   Brenan, *The Spanish Labyrinth* (New York, 1943),
   pp. 131-203.

9. For details of the Sanjurjo revolt and its implications, see Georges-Roux, *op. cit.*, p. 10; Juan Antonio Ansaldo, *Para Que? De Alfonso XIII a Juan III* (Buenos Aires, 1951), pp. 31-39.

Though this event is quite often dismissed as a reckless gesture on the part of faithful followers of the king, the important point to remember is that from this very moment the enemies of the Republic were in intimate contact with reactionary centers in France, Portugal, England and Italy. Furthermore, the upper class conspirators learned the primary revolutionary lesson: it is dangerous to play at insurrection. Four years later the same groups did not make the same mistakes.

10. Pierre Broué and Emile Témine, *La revolución y la guerra de España,* Vol. I (Mexico City, 1962), pp. 38-45 (French ed., Paris, 1961); Foltz, *op. cit.*, pp. 36-75; Hugh Thomas, *The Spanish Civil War* (New York, 1961), pp. 38-64.

11. Brenan, *op. cit.*, pp. 265-298.

12. Brenan, *op. cit.*, p. 147; Sedwick, *op. cit.*, p. 122.

It was doubly tragic that a senseless act of violence by a handful of illiterate peasants triggered an equally mindless deed of counter-violence. Whatever may have been the weaknesses of Manuel Azaña, he was a man who abhorred bloodshed. In 1931, after the first disturbances which marked the birth of the Republic and led to the burning of churches, Azaña refused to use the police power of the state, declaring that he would rather see all the churches of Spain burn than risk the life of a single republican.

See in this connection, Georges-Roux, *op. cit.*, pp. 21-25.

13. The elections of 1933 were more than a parliamentary
    contest. The oligarchy knew exactly what was at stake:
    the translation of economic power into political con-
    trol by a conscious perversion of the electoral process.
    In hundreds of villages and small towns the ballot was
    only formally free. The illiterate peasants (65% of
    Spain could neither read nor write) were told that if
    the landowners' candidate did not win, they would be
    thrown off the land. This system was not new to the
    Republic. It had thwarted any kind of democratizing
    process since the nineteenth century, and even had a
    name, *Caciquismo*. See Sedwick, *op. cit.*, p. 130; Roué
    & Témime, *op. cit.*, Vol. I, p. 76; Jackson, *op. cit.*, pp.
    98-121; de Madariaga, *op. cit.*, pp. 317-339.

14. This period in Spanish Republican history has earned
    the name, the *Bienio Negro*—the two black years. For
    those interested in comparative history, they corre-
    spond quite exactly to the same chronological epoch
    in Germany which witnessed the intrigues of Brüning,
    Von Papen, Hugenberg and the terrified petit bour-
    geoisie, all of which was prologue to Hitler's legal
    rise to supreme power in the Third Reich. A Spanish
    Hitler could not arise from the parliamentary cesspool
    because the Spanish working class fought back with
    the desperate courage that was so terribly lacking in
    Germany.

    An extensive coverage of the *Bienio Negro* is given
    by Jackson, *op. cit.*, pp. 121-148; Brenan, *op. cit.*, pp.
    265-297; Jellinek, *op. cit.*, pp. 144-167; Ramos Oliveira,
    op. cit., pp. 472-484; Dolores Ibarruri, *El Unico Cam-
    ino, Memorias de "la Pasionaria"* (Mexico City, 1963),
    pp. 149-157; Castro Delgado, *op. cit.*, pp. 145-204.

15. For the history of Spanish fascism prior to the out-
    break of the war in 1936, see Stanley Payne, *Falange,*

The History of Spanish Fascism (Stanford, 1961), *passim*: Brenan, *op. cit.*, pp. 298-316; Thomas, *op. cit.*, pp. 64-74; Foltz, *op. cit.*, pp. 60-88; Jellinek, *op. cit.*, pp. 275-299; Rama, *op. cit.*, pp. 193-197.

16. Georges-Roux, *op. cit.*, pp. 34-37; Ansaldo, *op. cit.*, pp. 63-75; Castro Delgado, *op. cit.*, pp. 239-252; Julio Alvarez del Vayo, *The Last Optimist* (New York, 1950), pp. 259-278.

17. Ansaldo, *op. cit.*, pp. 71-75; Thomas, *op. cit.*, pp. 95-110.

18. The Spanish army is a unique institution and all resemblances of it to the national armies of modern Europe are purely coincidental. After the breakup of the Spanish empire in the war of 1898, the Spanish army, apart from disastrous forays in North Africa, was primarily an organ of internal repression. Although the troubled events of 1934-36 led to the dominance of the purely putschist categories, its ranks contained a large number of decent republican spirits. They played a tragic, but doubly heroic role in the war of 1936-39. Many of the soldiers who genuinely wished to reform the Republic and who welcomed the disappearance of the monarchy were butchered in cold blood by the military conspirators of 1936.

For accounts of the role of the army, 1931-36, see Foltz, *op. cit.*, pp. 36-60; Jellinek, *op. cit.*, pp. 54-65; Ramos Oliveira, *op. cit.*, pp. 325-336; Rama, *op. cit.*, pp. 197-206, Brenan, *op. cit.*, pp. 57-78; Eduardo Fernández y González, *A Tragedia da Espanha de Felipe V a Francisco Franco* (Sao Paulo, 1947), pp. 366-414.

19. The history of the military conspiracy against the

Spanish Republic falls outside the scope of this study. Although the entire story has not yet been written, good accounts of it are given by Thomas, *op. cit.*, pp. 117-125; Jackson, *op. cit.*, pp. 196-231; Alvarez del Vayo, *Freedom's Battle* (New York, 1940), pp. 3-23. An invaluable analysis of the mythology surrounding the military rebellion is contained in Herbert R. Southworth, *Le Mythe de la Croisade de Franco* (Paris, 1964; Spanish ed., Paris, 1963. A revised English edition is forthcoming), *passim*. It should be pointed out that even today it is widely believed that the soldiers who betrayed their oath to the Second Republic did so in order to forestall a communist *coup d'état*. This assertion is the sheerest nonsense.

20. The text of the agreement signed between Spanish Rightists and the Italian Fascist Government, the famous Mussolini-Goicoechea Pact, was published by United Editorial Ltd. (London, 1938) under the title, *How Mussolini Provoked the Spanish Civil War*. Felipe Bertrán Guel, *Preparacion y Desarrollo del Alzamiento Nacional* (Valladolid, 1939) gives the most complete account of the conspiracy. See also Alvarez del Vayo, *Freedom's Battle*, p. 50; Ansaldo, *op. cit.*, p. 54. The work of Ansaldo is extremely revealing because as a pilot, it was his function to fly the conspirators to both foreign and domestic rendezvous.

21. The following chronology will set the Spanish events in the necessary context:

1934
Jan. 8:   Revolt against fascists in Portugal crushed
Feb. 6-7:   Stavisky riots in Paris

Feb. 11-15:	Civil war in Vienna
March 31:	Secret agreement between Spanish Rightists and Mussolini
June 30:	Hitler's Blood Purge
July 25:	Murder of Dolfuss
Sept. 18:	USSR joins League of Nations
Oct. 4-18:	Asturian uprising; Catalan uprising
Oct. 9:	Assassination of King Alexander and Foreign Minister Barthou in Marseilles
Dec. 1:	Assassination of Sergei Kirov
Dec. 5:	First clash of Italian troops with Ethiopian forces

1935

Jan. 7:	Laval promises Mussolini free hand in Ethiopia
May 2:	French-Russian military pact
June 7:	Stanley Baldwin Prime Minister of Great Britain
June 18:	Anglo-German naval agreement
July-Aug.:	Communist International adopts Popular Front strategy
Dec. 12:	Sian incident; Beginning of United Front strategy in Asia

1936

| Feb. 16: | Popular Front coalition wins Spanish elections. |

22. See note 14; Ibarruri, *op. cit.*, p. 156; Fernández y González, *op. cit.*, p. 410; Foltz, *op. cit.*, p. 23; Rama, *op. cit.*, pp. 164-175; Ansaldo, *op. cit.*, pp. 91-106; Jackson, *op. cit.*, pp. 135-150; Thomas, *op. cit.*, pp. 64-86.

23. Probably no subject is more booby-trapped than the

history of working class politics during the Second Republic. These parties, like all else in Spain, had an innate tendency toward fragmentization. Superimposed upon the regionalism was the tendency toward schism generated by strong personalities. The word "socialism" tended to change its meaning quite drastically as one moved from the bourgeois mentality of Basque workers to the quasi-nihilism of Barcelona and Cadiz. Probably only in Spain could Prieto, Besteiro and Francisco Largo Caballero belong to the same party. Until 1933 the dominant tendency of Spanish socialism was not much different from that of the British Labor Party or the French Socialists across the Pyrenees. Under the hammer blows of the Right and the irrepressible revolutionary fervor of the anarchists, Caballero and his supporters were driven into an insurrectionary mood. This changing psychology of the leadership and its mass following was not paralleled by an effort to build an organization capable of fulfilling in practice the revolutionary dreams of Caballero and his friends. It was this gap which provided the entrée for the Spanish Communist Party and schismatic groups to the "left" of the communists, such as those following Joaquin Maurín and Andrés Nin.

Castro Delgado, a rival of Caballero, but an astute observer of Spanish realities, wrote the following:

"The left wing forces looked to Don Paco. Don

Paco was Don Francisco Largo Caballero, an honest man, a good husband and a good father. He had arrived at the leadership of the Socialist Party like many employees become the head of a business: by seniority. But this Don Paco, who was an expert labor bureaucrat, knew nothing of revolutions, what they were or how to make them.

Some of his followers began to call him 'the
Spanish Lenin,' which was a sacrilege and stupid,
as well as illusion created in desperation."

—*op. cit.*, p. 200.

Caballero did not learn how to read until he was 24,
and he read none of the classics of Marx and Lenin
until he was jailed in 1934. Many liberal writers, such
as de Madariaga, have blamed the 1936 rebellion on
the policies of Largo Caballero. See de Madariaga,
op. cit., pp. 367-380.

See also Ibarruri, *op. cit.*, pp. 153-155; Brenan, *op.
cit.*, pp. 221-223, 302-313; Alvarez del Vayo, *The Last
Optimist*, pp. 198-210, 262, 266; Broué & Témime, *op.
cit.*, Vol. I, pp. 59-69.

24. Castro Delgado, *op. cit.*, pp. 139-143, 182-199; Ibarruri,
op. cit., pp. 148-155.

It is well nigh impossible to determine the organized
strength of the Spanish Communist Party with any
degree of accuracy. It is probable that in 1933 its
membership was close to 3,000, but in the November
elections of that year it polled 400,000 votes and
actually won a seat in the Cortes from Málaga. The
Málaga election, forgotten in the Rightist sweep, was
important because there the Communist candidate
won in virtue of an anti-fascist coalition agreement, a
preview of the Popular Front policy of 1936. It is a
poignant footnote to the tragic history of the 1930's
that the Spanish Communist Party advocated an anti-
fascist coalition policy when such an idea was anathema to the dogmatists controlling the Communist
International. The rival Socialist Party during the
period of Communist Party growth declined from
80,000 members to 60,000. Communist strength was
scattered, being strongest in southern Andalusia and
among the northern coal miners.

25. Ibarruri, *op. cit.*, p. 155; Castro Delgado, *op. cit.*, p. 201; Brenan, *op. cit.*, pp. 274, 285; Broué & Témime, *op. cit.*, Vol. I, pp. 59-69.

There can be no question but that Caballero's stubborn refusal to draw the powerful anarchist trade unions into the Alianza was motivated by his fear that his beloved UGT might lose members to the more radical anarchist syndicates. It must be remembered also that trade union rivalry in Spain had very little to do with control of union dues. Two hostile world views were in conflict, and on many occasions issues were settled with pistols.

26. Alvarez del Vayo, *The Last Optimist*, pp. 260-264; Thomas, *op. cit.*, p. 77.

27. No comprehensive, documented history of the 1934 disorders in Spain exists. Historical fragments of what was surely one of the most important proletarian actions since the Russian Revolution are gathered in the following: Jackson, *op. cit.*, pp. 148-169; Broué & Témime, *op. cit.*, Vol. I, p. 63; Castro Delgado, *op. cit.*, 201-205; Brenan, *op. cit.*, pp. 281-291; Ibarruri, *op. cit*, pp. 156-161; Ansaldo, *op. cit.*, pp. 78-93; Thomas, *op. cit.*, pp. 74-95; Jellinek, *op. cit.*, pp. 167-195; de Madariaga, *op. cit.*, pp. 330-339.

When the time comes to write a complete history of the European working class between the two world wars, then and only then will the full importance of the Asturian Commune be recognized. Legalistic liberals such as de Madariaga have asserted that with the revolt of 1934, the Spanish Republicans lost all moral grounds for condemning the rebellion of the generals in 1936.

This Jesuitical argument seeks to blur the distinction between the murderer and his victim. Robles and his allies had been preparing to assassinate the Republic for years. Months before the miners fired the first pistol, Rightist envoys in Rome had committed high treason against the Republic by accepting guns and cash from Mussolini.

It is important also to note that a considerable number of middle class politicians with no sympathy for any of the working class parties warned the President of the Republic, Alcalá Zamora, that the entry of the sworn enemies of the Constitution into the cabinet would mean the end of legal means of resistance.

Thus the Asturian miners take their place with the barricade fighters of Vienna in that pantheon of heroes whose common sense and deep consciousness of proletarian dignity inspired them to die rather than submit to either the blandishments or machine guns of fascism.

28. Calvo Sotelo was the young brilliant Finance Minister under the dictator Primo de Rivera who, in 1934, brought a great deal of brains and style to the ultra Right. For further data on the sinister role of Calvo Sotelo, see Thomas, *op. cit.*, pp. 6-10; Ramos Oliveira, *op. cit.*, pp. 540, 547, 553, 566; Jellinek, *op. cit.*, pp. 244-262.

29. An editorial in the underground Communist Party newspaper, *Norte Rojo,* published immediately after the Asturian defeat, said:

> "We have been defeated, but we have not been conquered. The working class, because of lack of leadership and organization, has not been able to develop all of its power. It can do much more. It can bring about the triumph of the revolution.

The counter-revolution can do no more than it
has done in Asturias. The Spanish October has
been like 1905 in Russia. Still to come is the
November, 1917."

—Castro Delgado, *op. cit.*, p. 219.

The historical allusion cuts both ways. After 1905
in Russia, the Old Order quenched the flames of
revolution and began a desperate modernization of
the empire that was interrupted by the outbreak of
World War I. The Spanish Right, gloating over the
corpses of its victims, far from undertaking any struc-
tural reforms, attempted in its blind and stupid fury
to turn the clock even farther back.

30. It is an extraordinary fact of Spanish politics of this
period that between the crushing of the revolts of 1934
and the dissolution of the Cortes in 1935—the prologue to the Popular Front electoral agreement—the
Spanish Right began to break up into fragments.
These were represented by the rivalries of the groups
around Calvo Sotelo and Gil Robles and the disputes
between the convinced monarchists and the gunmen
controlling the Falange. It is probable also, though
there is no iron-clad evidence, that the Vatican, disturbed by events in Germany and Austria, drew back
from a clerical-fascist experiment in Spain. While old
and new groups of politicians played musical chairs,
and engaged in a consciousless plundering of the public treasury, the hard core of conspirators continued
to plan for a military takeover. The center of this plot
was the group around General Sanjurjo in Portugal.

The civilian executive in Spain's government was
Gil Robles in the Ministry of War. Generals Franco,
Mola and Goded were the primary figures in the of-
ficer corps. When the elections were announced for

February of 1936, the Right was confident of victory. How little did they understand the psychology of their intended victims!

It is highly probable that another factor which the over-confident Right ignored was the magnificent effort made by Manuel Azaña, the weary symbol of the battered Republic, to draw the frightened middle class away from fascism. Perhaps a million Castillians listened to his great electoral oratory. The best accounts of this interregnum are to be found in Ramos Oliveira, *op. cit.*, pp. 517-567; Jellinek, *op. cit.*, pp. 181-229; Jackson, *op. cit.*, pp. 169-196.

31. It is highly ironic that it was the well-publicized mistreatment of the thousands of prisoners which created the conditions for the electoral defeat of the Right. The anarchist masses could never have been moved to political action by the tepid social program proposed by the coalition parties. To release their comrades from the torture chambers they would do anything, including vote. And it was their votes that won the election.

Proletarian unity was not absolutely complete. The ultra Left, including groups of schismatic communists sympathetic to Trotsky, such as the followers of Nin and Maurín, stood aloof. Trotsky's views on anti-fascist coalitions are set down in his secret diary. In February of 1935, he wrote:

"Under these conditions the Stalinists form a bloc with the Radicals 'against fascism' and try to force the Socialists to join them—a windfall the latter never even dared to dream of. Like half-trained monkeys, some Stalinists even now keep on grumbling about the bloc: what we need is not parliamentary deals with the Radicals, but a 'people's front'

against fascism! One feels as if one were reading an
official paper from the madhouse at Charenton! A
parliamentary bloc with the Radicals, no matter
how criminal from the point of view of the interests of socialism, makes—or at least made—political
sense as a device in the electoral and parliamentary
strategy of democratic reformers. But what possible
sense could there be in an extra-parliamentary bloc
with a purely parliamentary party which by its very
social composition is incapable of any extra-parliamentary mass action whatsoever? The bourgeois
elite of the party is scared to death of its own mass
base. To accept once every four years the votes of
the peasants, petty tradesmen and officials—to this
Herriot magnanimously agrees. But to lead them
into an open struggle means to conjure up spirits of
which he is much more afraid than he is of fascism.
The so-called 'popular front,' i.e., the bloc with the
Radicals for extra-parliamentary action, is the most
criminal mockery of the people that the working-
class parties have permitted themselves since the
war—and they have permitted themselves a great
deal."
—Leon Trotsky, *Trotsky's Secret Diary in Exile,
1935* (Cambridge, Mass., 1958), pp. 17-18.
For an analysis of the psychology of the ultra revolutionaries of Spain, see Franz Borkenau, *The Spanish
Cockpit* (London, 1937), *passim;* Brenan, *op. cit.*,
pp. 223-254, 274-296, 324-328; V. Richards, *Lessons of
the Spanish Revolution, 1936-1939* (London, 1953),
passim.

An extremely perceptive critique of working class
politics in Spain has been written by the Falangist
historian, Maximiano García Venero, *Historia de las
Internacionales en España* (Madrid, 1957), IV vols.
In the Spring of 1937 the hostility between the POUM

and the Republican Government, supported by the Communists and Socialists, led to a week of street fighting in Barcelona. See also note 78 below.

32. Ibarruri, *op. cit.*, pp. 168-189; Castro Delgado, *op. cit.*, pp. 234-238.

33. For the electoral program of the Popular Front, see *International Press Correspondence, Special Spain Number*, pp. 597-598. For an analysis of the campaign, see Broué & Témime, *op. cit.*, Vol. I, pp. 75-98.

34. Ibarruri, *op. cit.*, pp. 202-207.

35. For the last phases of the military conspiracy against the Republic, see Broué & Témime, *op. cit.*, Vol. I, pp. 80-90; Ibarruri, *op. cit.*, pp. 228-241; Thomas, *op. cit.*, pp. 95-131. Additional details can be found in Bertrán Güel, *op. cit.*, p. 76; Ansaldo, *op. cit.*, pp. 115-129.

36. The extreme disorder throughout the country, particularly in the months preceding the uprising, was used by the rebel apologists as a justification for what they had been plotting since 1932. The American ambassador to Republican Spain, Mr. Claude Bowers, in his book, *My Mission to Spain* (New York, 1954), gives irrefutable evidence that the Left parties planned no violence against the State. Falangist provocateurs, however, well armed by the German legations, kept the country boiling.

37. Genevieve Tabouis, *They Call Me Cassandra* (New York, 1942), p. 297; E. N. Dzelepy, *The Spanish Plot* (London, 1937), chap. 3.

38. Bertrán Güel, *op. cit.*, p. 123.

39. Jellinek, *op. cit.*, p. 286.

40. Felix Morrow, *Revolution and Counter-Revolution in Spain* (New York, 1938), pp. 15-23.

    Rarely has the indecision of political figures had more deadly consequences than the hesitation of the Spanish bourgeois politicians when first confronted with the well-advertised fact that the army was in open rebellion. Since this fatal Hamletism of the Spanish Republicans of 1936, similar events have taken place in other parts of the "underdeveloped" world.

    The overthrow of Arbenz in Guatemala, of Goulart in Brazil, the collapse of Sukarno in Indonesia, and a number of other coups in Latin America, are cases in point. In each instance the dilemma arises from either the fear of the people by the government or lack of confidence of a bureaucracy that has no popular base. Compare this sorry record with the successful defense of Madrid discussed below, or the triumph of Fidel Castro in Cuba.

41. For the balance of fighting in the first weeks of the war, see Thomas, *op. cit.*, chap. 17; Jackson, *op. cit.*, chaps. 14 & 15; Cisneros, *op. cit.*, Vol. II, pp. 267-282; Luis María de Lojendio, *Operaciones Militares de la Guerra de España, 1936-1939* (Barcelona, 1940), chaps. 1 & 2.

42. Cisneros, *op. cit.*, Vol. II, p. 284; Lojendio, *op. cit.*, pp. 23-54.

    Details of the early German intervention which secured for Franco a base of operations in Spain is contained in the *Report of the Subcommittee on the Spanish Question*, Security Council Official Records, United Nations (New York, 1946). Also of great interest are the statements of four German generals involved in these operations. The reports of these officers, Bamler, Remer, Jaenecke and Böhme, were published as a supplement to *New Times*, no. 13 (Moscow, July 1, 1946).

A complete record of German intervention throughout the course of the war is found in *Documents on German Foreign Policy, 1918-1945*, Series D, Vol. III, Germany and the Spanish Civil War, 1936-1939 (Department of State, Washington, D.C., 1950), hereinafter referred to as *German Documents*.

43. H. R. D. Greaves and David Thomson, *The Truth about Spain* (London, 1938), p. 58.

One of the sources of the Spanish Republican Fleet's difficulties was the fact that these ships had been seized for the Republic by the crews who remained loyal to the Government; in many cases the officers who wished to support the rebellion were killed and thrown overboard. To the British Admiralty this was the sin of sins. The Admiralty's powerful political weight was exerted from the first moment of the war on the side of Franco.

44. The origin of the non-intervention policy, a prime case of appeasement, has been thoroughly studied in many standard works on the diplomacy of the period. The early appraisal of Frederick L. Schuman still stands as the definitive summary of those diplomatic decisions:

"As soon as minutes and memoirs are made public, it will become possible for historians of the future to reconstruct in detail one of the most diverting diplomatic farces of modern times: the proceed-

ings of the London Non-Intervention Committee
through which all the states of Europe supervised
intervention in the Spanish war. Archaeologists and
classicists of days to come may find evidence in
these records that the civilization of the 20th
century was, even in its decadence, not lacking
in humor. They may conclude, however, that the
quality and purport of the humor were in themselves unmistakable symptoms of decline . . . ."
    —*Europe on the Eve* (New York, 1939), p. 283.
For further details on Blum's policy, see Dzelepy,
op. cit., passim; Pierre Cot, *The Triumph of Treason*
(New York, 1944), *passim.* The texts of Leon Blum's
speeches and writings on the Spanish conflict are in
Leon Blum, L'Oeuvre, Vol. I, *1934-1937;* Vol. II,
1937-1940 (Paris, 1965).

Despite all efforts to make his decisions palatable
to a new generation of Frenchmen, it would appear
that the decision with respect to Spain represented a
failure of socialist morality and nerve. Once the first
step had been taken, French policy remained forever
bound to that of the appeasers in London. A masterly
analysis of the British Conservative attitude towards
Spain will be found in Margaret George, *The Warped
Vision, British Foreign Policy, 1933-1939* (Pittsburgh,
1965), pp. 93-115.

45. The record of Italian intervention in the Spanish conflict is scattered through a dozen histories of the war.
It is treated in great detail in the works of Jellinek,
Thomas and Jackson, previously cited. Manuel Tuñon
de Lara's *Storia della Republica e della Guerra Civile
in Spagna* (Rome, 1966) also has a complete account
of the Italian government's contributions to Franco's
victory. The diplomatic double-dealing and the chi-

canery of the Italians is fully set forth in *Ciano's Diplomatic Papers* (London, 1948) and in *Ciano's Diary, 1937-1938* (London, 1952).

46. One of the least studied aspects of the Spanish conflict is the nefarious role of Portugal. For details, see Carlos Prieto, *The Spanish Front* (London, 1936), p. 78 et seq.; London *News Chronicle*, August 25, 1936 and November 1, 1936; and Dante A. Puzzo, *Spain and the Great Powers, 1936-1941* (New York, 1962), pp. 69-73, 108-109, 121, 123. Puzzo's book also contains good summaries of all foreign intervention. Also of great value is "Hispanicus," *Foreign Intervention in Spain* (London, 1937), *passim.*

47. See Schuman, *op. cit., passim;* George, *op. cit., passim.* For a useful bibliography of the diplomacy of the inter-war years, see my selection in the University of Pittsburgh's new edition of Etienne Mantoux, *The Carthaginian Peace* (Pittsburgh, 1964), pp. 214-231. Perhaps the most useful summaries to this vast material are Gaetano Salvemini, *Prelude to World War II* (New York, 1954), and D. F. Fleming, *The Cold War and Its Origins, 1917-1960*, 2 vols. (New York, 1961).

48. All of the Churchillian quotes are taken from his *Great Contemporaries* (New York, 1937). For Churchill's slightly later thoughts on Spain, see his *Step by Step, 1936-1939* (New York, 1939). The "naval person" awoke to the folly of British Spanish policy when the victory of the Axis had been practically consummated.

49. Robert Sencourt, *Spain's Ordeal* (London, 1940), p. 149.

50. The most objective analysis of terror on both sides is that of Jackson, *op. cit.*, pp. 276-310. See also Broué & Témime, *op. cit.*, Vol. I, pp. 209-214.

51. Discussion of Soviet participation in the Spanish conflict is scattered throughout hundreds of volumes that have been written about this war. The central fact, however, is very simple. Drawn into the non-intervention pact for the reasons cited in the text, the Soviet government, confronted by the massive intervention of Germany, Italy and Portugal, reversed itself and began to assist the Republic. Had the USSR remained neutral, the fascists would have won the war not later than mid-November, 1936. The fundamental reason for the reversal is as given in the text.

   For an analysis of the Soviet participation, see the relevant sections of Jellinek, Thomas, Jackson, Schuman, Puzzo and Salvemini, cited above. Interesting sidelights on this are given by the following: Alvarez del Vayo, Ibarruri, Broué & Témime, Ramos Oliveira, Cisneros, Castro Delgado, García Venero and Borkenau, cited above. Highly "academic" studies are provided by David T. Cattell, *Communism and the Spanish Civil War* (Berkeley, 1955) and *Soviet Diplomacy and the Spanish Civil War* (Berkeley, 1956).

   To understand how the Spanish conflict impinged upon Soviet society in general, the indispensable work is Ilya Ehrenburg, *Memoirs: 1921-1941*, Vol. II (Cleveland, 1964). This is perhaps the most melancholy book ever written on the subject. Mikhail Koltsov's *Ispanskij Dnevnik* (*Spanish Diary*) (Moscow, 1957) is extremely useful. This has been translated into Spanish. A definitive account of Soviet involvement in the Spanish conflict is now being prepared by Soviet scholars. For the role of the Soviet mission in the crucial struggle for Madrid, see my book, *The Struggle for Madrid, The Central Epic of the Spanish Conflict, 1936-1937* (New York, 1958).

52. An extremely large literature has grown up about the International Brigades. The important works are: Luigi Longo, *Le brigate internationali in Spagna* (Rome, 1956); Lisa Lindbaek, *Internationella Brigaden* (Stockholm, 1939); Pietro Nenni, *Spagna* (Rome, 1958); Randolfo Pacciardi, *Il Battaglione Garibaldi* (Rome, 1945); Ludwig Renn, *Der Spanische Kreig* (Berlin, 1956); Arthur Landis, *The Abraham Lincoln Brigade* (New York, 1966); Alvah Bessie, *Men in Battle; The Story of Americans in Spain* (New York, 1939); Edwin Rolfe, *The Lincoln Battalion* (New York, 1939); William Rust, *Britons in Spain* (London, 1939); Max Wullschleger (ed.), *Schweizer Kämpfen in Spanien* (Zurich, 1939); Theodore Balk, *La Quatorzième* (Madrid, 1937).

Of great documentary value is the collective work, *Pasaremos, Deutsche Antifaschisten im National Revolutionaren Krieg des Spanischen Volkes,* produced by the Social Science Faculty of the Friedrich Engels Military Academy (Berlin, D.D.R., 1966), hereinafter cited as *Pasaremos.*

The primary contribution of the International Brigades was made during the battles for Madrid. For complete details, see Colodny, *op. cit., passim.*

53. Georgi Dimitrov, *Spain and the People's Front* (New York, 1937).

54. Ibarruri, *op. cit.,* p. 315; Colodny, *op. cit.,* pp. 162-166.

One of the incredible myths which fuses the trag-
edies of Spain and the Soviet Union asserts that all of
the Soviet officers who survived the rigors of war in
Spain were shot upon their return home by Joseph
Stalin. Though many perished in the purges, the
aforementioned list should explode this filthy legend
once and for all.

55. The time-tables of Nazi intervention in Spain are
given in *Pasaremos*. The German General Staff,
though reluctant to become too deeply involved in
Spain, quickly saw the value of the Spanish arena
for training its officers and testing its equipment. The
survivors of this post-graduate period all achieved
high commands in Hitler's army.

For details of the political maneuvers of the Ger-
mans in Spain, see *German Documents, passim.*
Useful additional insights are provided by Werner
Beumelburg, *Kämpf um Spanien* (Berlin, 1939); Gen-
eral Alfredo Kindelán, *Mis Cuadernos de Guerra*
(Madrid, 1945); Karl Silex, *Der Marsch auf Madrid*
(Leipzig, 1937); The Journal, *Die Wehrmacht*
Berlin).

56. Ibarruri, *op. cit.*, pp. 310-315. For fuller bibliographical details, see Colodny, *op. cit.*, pp. 176-205.

57. When the Russian missions were established in Madrid and Barcelona, Soviet films of the Russian civil
war were shown over and over again to the Spanish
militia. The Soviet advisers, many of whom had participated in the dramatic events of October, 1917, and
the Russian civil war, tended to think of Madrid in
terms of Leningrad. Had Spain possessed the vast

spaces of Mother Russia, the Russian tactics might have been more successful.

58. The details of Soviet political advice to the Spanish government are scattered through scores of books. The most useful are those of Castro Delgado, Cisneros, Ibarruri, Alvarez del Vayo, Ramos Oliveira, Ehrenburg, Broué & Témime, and Cattell, previously cited. Additional information, much of it critical of Soviet intervention in the political domain, is to be found in Eudocio Ravines, *The Yenan Way* (New York, 1951); Elena de la Souchère, *An Explanation of Spain* (New York, 1965); and Ypsilon, *Pattern for World Revolution* (Chicago, 1947).

59. Colodny, *op. cit.*, chap. 2, "The Road from Toledo," pp. 11-37; Tuñon de Lara, *op. cit.*, pp. 483-505.

60. Manuel Chavez Nogales, *Heroes and Beasts of Spain* (New York, 1937), has painted the most vivid descriptions of these actions. See also Ramon J. Sender, *Counter-Attack in Spain* (New York, 1937); Castro Delgado, *op. cit.*, pp. 262-307; J. M. Blazquez, *I Helped Build an Army* (London, 1939), *passim;* Henry Buckley, *Life and Death of the Spanish Republic* (London, 1939), chap. 27.

61. Sencourt, *op. cit.*, pp. 141-146.

62. Jay Allen of the Chicago *Tribune* cabled a full account of the Badajoz massacre. It has been published separately as *The Crime of Badajoz* (New York, 1937). Picasso's mural has made the crime of Guernica immortal.

63. Franco's emergence from one among equals to un-

disputed dictator of rebel Spain was due in large measure to the death of General Sanjurjo, who was killed while flying from Portugal to Spain; to the death of General Mola, also in a mysterious plane accident; and to the unqualified support of the Nazis. Furthermore, as the commander of the Army of Africa, Franco controlled from the beginning the deadliest military weapon in the hands of the rebels. A synthetic political following was then created by *diktat*. The Republic remained fragmented ideologically and hence was never able to coordinate its potentially stronger forces. This deficiency, along with the terrible disparity in armament, crippled the anti-fascist coalition.

64. Peter Merin, *Spain between Death and Birth* (New York, 1938), p. 203. On the recruiting of Moors in French Africa, see also Cisneros, *op. cit.*, Vol. II, p. 312.

65. The quote is from a nineteenth-century observer, Karl Marx. Throughout the conflict the capacity of resistance and the creativity of the Spanish people was under-estimated by the politicians. Manuel Azaña, the President, was a defeatist in his heart from the very beginning. Prieto, a man of great intelligence, who held key positions in the Ministry of Defense, could never bring himself to believe in the implications of socialist rhetoric. It was the officers who rose directly from the people who created the miracle at Madrid. They were ably supported by a handful of capable soldiers who remained loyal to the Republic, above all by Vicente Rojo, who rose to become Chief of the General Staff.

66. Castro Delgado, *op. cit.*, chaps. 5 & 6. Although it has romantic exaggerations, Ernest Hemingway's play,

The Fifth Column (London, 1938), recreates the atmosphere of beleaguered Madrid. Despite the manhunts, however, the Republic never purged either the government apparatus or the High Command of concealed fascist sympathizers. The results of this failure were catastrophic.

67. Lázaro Somoza-Silva, *El General Miaja: Biografía de un Héroe* (Mexico City, 1944), p. 183.

68. For an exhaustive analysis of the fascist mythology concerning the origins of the Spanish conflict, see the master work of Herbert R. Southworth, *op. cit.*, *passim.*

69. For the attitude of the French Right towards the Spanish conflict, see Tabouis, *op. cit.*, *passim;* Cot, *op. cit.*, *passim;* André Simone, *Men of Europe* (New York, 1941), chap. 5; A. Simone, *J'Accuse! The Men Who Betrayed France* (New York, 1940), *passim;* Pertinax, *The Gravediggers of France* (New York, 1944), *passim;* L. B. Namier, *Europe in Decay: A Study in Disintegration, 1936-1940* (London, 1950), *passim.*

70. There is a growing body of literature concerning the impact of the Spanish conflict on the mind and conscience of the world. The most valuable books are Allen Guttmann, *Wound in the Heart, America and the Spanish Civil War* (New York, 1962); K. W. Watkins, *Britain Divided* (London, 1963); Peter Stansky and William Abrahams, *Journey to the Frontier, Julian Bell and John Cornford: Their Lives and the 1930's* (London, 1966); Hugh D. Ford, *A Poet's War: British Poets in the Spanish Civil War* (London, 1965); Alvah Bessie (ed.), *The Heart of Spain* (New

York, 1952); John M. Muste, *Say That We Saw Spain Die, Literary Consequences of the Spanish Civil War* (Seattle, 1966).

What these books accomplish for the English-speaking world Ehrenburg's *Memoirs* and *Pasaremos* achieve for the Soviet and German worlds. The literary testaments of Simone de Beauvoir, Jean Paul Sartre, Albert Camus and Louis Aragon reflect the tragic impact of Spain on the French mind.

71. A detailed analysis of the Madrid battles will be found in my book, *The Struggle for Madrid,* along with abundant bibliographical material.

72. In addition to the details given in Colodny, *op. cit.,* see Landis, *op. cit.* (chap. on Jarama), and Renn, *op. cit.,* pp. 174-196. This is an indispensable source. 3200 American volunteers served in Spain. Of these, 1500 were killed in action. Over 1600 were wounded. Of the survivors, over 400 were killed fighting in World War II.

73. Cisneros, *op. cit.,* Vol. II, pp. 277-390; Colodny, *op. cit.,* pp. 128-143, 231-238.

74. Herbert L. Matthews, *Two Wars and More to Come* (New York, 1937), p. 264. For Matthews' later reflections on the Guadalajara campaign, see his *The Yoke and the Arrows, A Report on Spain* (New York, 1957, 1961), pp. 213-227.

75. These reflections are taken from Gustav Regler's magnificent novel, *The Great Crusade* (New York, 1939).

76. For details of British policy during the northern

campaign, see "The Unknown Diplomat" (E. N. Dzelepy), *Britain in Spain* (London, 1939), pp. 59-80.

77. For the military and political aspects of the Basque tragedy, see Castro Delgado, *op. cit.*, pp. 514-538; Jackson, *op. cit.*, pp. 375-392; Ramos Oliveira, *op. cit.*, pp. 620-629; Cisneros, *op. cit.*, Vol. II, pp. 409-427; Thomas, *op. cit.*, chaps. 50, 51, 54, 55, 56.

78. Concerning the Barcelona tragedy, see George Orwell, *Homage to Catalonia* (London, 1938), *passim;* Cisneros, *op. cit.*, Vol. II, pp. 390-394; Agustin Souchy, *The Tragic Week in May* (Barcelona, 1937), *passim;* Borkenau, *op. cit.*, pp. 173-257.

On May 11, 1937, General Faupel wired the German Foreign Ministry from Salamanca: "As for the disorders in Barcelona, Franco informed me that the street fighting had been started by his agents. As Nicolás Franco further told me, they had in all some thirteen agents in Barcelona. One of these had given the information a considerable time ago that the tension between the Anarchists and Communists was so great in Barcelona that they would guarantee fighting to break out there."

—*German Documents*, no. 254.

79. The *Deutschland* was bombed on May 29, 1937 while in the harbor of the rebel-held island of Ibiza. The Republican aviators considered the *Deutschland* to be a hostile vessel. The German government claimed that it was on non-intervention patrol, a claim sustained by British and French diplomacy. In revenge, the battleship turned its great guns on the little town of Almería and destroyed it. See *German Documents*, nos. 267 through 285. Nothing quite like this will

happen again until the events in the Gulf of Tonkin in 1965.

80. Colodny, *op. cit.*, pp. 145-147; Renn, *op. cit.*, pp. 299-318; *Pasaremos,* pp. 125-131; Cisneros, *op. cit.*, Vol. II, pp. 402-404.

81. Soviet supply ships sailing from Odessa to Valencia and Barcelona, as well as other ships charted by the Spanish Republic, had to run the gauntlet of Italian submarines. Fascist spies in the Dardenelles kept the Italian Admiralty informed concerning the passage of Soviet shipping. When enough French and British ships had also been sunk, the democracies reacted with the convocation of the Nyon Conference. A few unambiguous threats to sink the "pirate" submarines were sufficient to prevent the further sinking of Anglo-French vessels. See Puzzo, *op. cit.*, pp. 195-200; "Unknown Diplomat," *op. cit.*, pp. 145-158; *German Documents,* nos. 413, 418; *Ciano's Diary,* p. 88. A searching investigation of the naval and maritime aspects of the Spanish conflict is now in preparation by Willard Frank.

82. Jackson, *op. cit.*, pp. 360-413. Contrast the spirit of despair with the portrayal of Madrid a few months before. See particularly Vincent Sheean, *Not Peace But a Sword* (New York, 1939), chap. 4.

83. The chaos which grew out of anarchist domination of Catalonia nowhere had a more deadly effect on the war than on the neighboring Aragon front. Not only did the militia units fail to press their advantage of numbers in offensive operations, they neglected completely the work of fortification. This military inactivity completely sapped the early morale of these amateur columns. In the first weeks of summer, 1937,

they actually played soccer matches with Falangist units from the besieged towns.

For details of the Republic's abortive offensive against Saragossa, see Cisneros, *op. cit.*, Vol. II, pp. 410-426; Renn, *op. cit.*, pp. 318-320; Castro Delgado, *op. cit.*, pp. 562-569; Tuñon de Lara, *op. cit.*, pp. 583-617.

84. For details of the Asturian campaign, see Castro Delgado, *op. cit.*, pp. 534-539, 572-585; Ibarruri, *op. cit.*, pp. 352-356; Jackson, *op. cit.*, pp. 375-392.

85. For details of the Teruel campaign, see Renn, *op. cit.*, pp. 321-322; Castro Delgado, *op. cit.*, chap. 13; Jackson, *op. cit.*, pp. 398-400; Thomas, *op. cit.*, pp. 504-517; *Pasaremos*, pp. 146-152.

86. Harold Cardozo, *March of a Nation* (New York, 1937), p. 18. Cardozo, who was sympathetic to the Franco cause and followed the triumphal march of the rebels through southern Spain, said with reference to the fuel supplies of the rebels: ". . . The Nationalist Government was amply supplied with petrol on credit. This was due to the fact that intelligent financiers had realized that the Nationalists were going to win, and that the Nationalists would pay."

Robert Sencourt adds: ". . . Not one of the governments behind non-intervention brought up, nor did the United States bring up, the question of petrol supplies. . . . Franco's own petrol came across the sea. In spite of Washington's insistence on neutrality, it was generously supplied by Standard Oil. It is interesting to note that the question of petrol, on which the duration of the war depended, was kept out of the newspapers of every country." (*op. cit.*, p. 351)

For further details bearing on the German decisions to meet materièl requirements of Franco's armies, see also *German Documents, passim;* Manfred Merkes, *Die deutsche Politik gegenüber dem spanischen Bürgerkrieg, 1936-1939* (Bonn, 1961), *passim;* Foltz, *op. cit.,* p. 52. For the Italian contributions, see the two *Ciano* references above.

87. For the details of the Aragon campaign, see Renn, *op. cit.,* pp. 323-330; Castro Delgado, *op. cit.,* chap. 14; Thomas, *op. cit.,* pp. 517-532; Cisneros, *op. cit.,* Vol. II, pp. 435-439; General Vicente Rojo, *Alerta los Pueblos! Estudio Politico-Militar del Periodo Final de la Guerra Española* (Buenos Aires, 1939), pp. 13-39; Tuñon de Lara, *op. cit.,* pp. 617-657; *German Documents,* nos. 546, 548, 559, 578; *Ciano's Diary,* pp. 86-96.

88. The sordid sequence of events through which the Nationalist "patriot" Generalissimo Franco was pressured to surrender the mineral rights of Spain to Hitler can be followed step by step by a careful perusal of the correspondence between the German diplomatic and military representatives in Spain and Berlin. See *German Documents,* nos. 205, 218, 219, 272, 336, 381, 386, 390, 391, 397, 401, 454, 455, 463, 464, 470, 472, 473, 475, 479, 486, 491-540, 507, 529, 561, 591, 655, 676, 684, 695, 701, 754, 773, 783, 786.

89. Alvarez del Vayo, *The Last Optimist,* pp. 300-304; *German Documents,* nos. 548, 549, 572, 573, 585, 587; Simone, *Men of Europe,* p. 169; Simone, *J'Accuse!* pp. 215-232; *Ciano's Diary,* p. 89.

90. *Ciano's Diplomatic Papers,* chaps. 14, 15, 16; Schu-

man, *op. cit.*, chaps. 7, 8, 9, 10; George, *op. cit.*, pp. 165-217; "Unknown Diplomat," *op. cit.*, chaps. 11, 12, 13.

91. Ramos Oliveira, *op. cit.*, p. 631.

92. "Unknown Diplomat," *op. cit.*, p. 194. The air raids in Catalonia actually disturbed the German government more than it did the British. See *German Documents*, nos. 594, 600, 617, 618.

93. Simone, *Men of Europe*, pp. 168-170.

94. Ramos Oliveira, *op. cit.*, pp. 610-613; Rojo, *loc. cit.*

95. Only the Ebro campaign has produced a mass of literature comparable to that concerning the battles at Madrid. This extraordinary battle was initiated by the same units that had held the Spanish capital at such great odds. See Castro Delgado, *op. cit.*, pp. 669-675; *Pasaremos*, pp. 164-185; Sheean, *op. cit.*, chap. 11; Cisneros, *op. cit.*, Vol. II, p. 439; Jackson, *op. cit.*, pp. 454-456; Zugazagoitia, *op. cit.*, pp. 430-432; Lojendio, *op. cit.*, pp. 398-436; Thomas, *op. cit.*, pp. 544-554; General Vicente Rojo, *España Heroica* (Buenos Aires, 1942), pp. 163-197; Julián Henriquez Caubín, *La Batalla del Ebro* (Mexico City, 1944), *passim.*

96. Among the most fascinating sources bearing on the bitter resistance of Spaniards in Franco's territory are the reports of German diplomatic and military representatives in rebel Spain. See *German Documents*, nos. 586, 628.

97. *German Documents*, nos. 656, 657, 658, 659, 660, 665, 668.

98. For the questions bearing on the withdrawal of foreign volunteers, see *German Documents*, nos. 620, 630, 632, 637, 638, 672, 675, 685, 701; Castro Delgado, *op. cit.*, pp. 675-682; Sheean, *op. cit.*, chap. 6.

99. Thomas, *op. cit.*, p. 558; Jackson, *op. cit.*, p. 462; Castro Delgado, *op. cit.*, p. 682.

100. For the Catalonian campaign, see Lojendio, *op. cit.*, pp. 535-597; Thomas, *op. cit.*, pp. 565-578; Rojo, *Alerte los Pueblos! passim; German Documents*, nos. 720, 740; Renn, *op. cit.*, pp. 367-370; Zugazagoitia, *op. cit.*, pp. 486-501.

101. Cisneros, *op. cit.*, Vol. II, pp. 445-456.

102. Concerning the presence of Soviet war materièl held in French ports, see *German Documents*, nos. 766, 777; Ramos Oliveira, *op. cit.*, p. 634.

103. See note 100.

104. Zugazagoitia, *op. cit.*, pp. 503-520.

105. The flight of the Spanish refugees across the winter-gripped Pyrenees awaits description by some new Tolstoy or Goya. See Ramos Oliveira, *op. cit.*, pp. 635-638; *Pasaremos*, pp. 262-265; Ehrenburg, *op. cit.*, pp. 460-466; Thomas, *op. cit.*, pp. 574-578.

106. Cisneros, *op. cit.*, Vol. II, pp. 463-465.

107. For the origins and development of the Casado *coup d'état*, see Zugazagoitia, *op. cit.*, pp. 532-590; Thomas, *op. cit.*, pp. 586-604; Ramos Oliveira, *op. cit.*, pp. 644-

685; Segismundo Casado, *The Last Days of Madrid* (London, 1939), *passim;* Alvarez del Vayo, *The Last Optimist,* pp. 304-306; Castro Delgado, *op. cit.,* pp. 729-785; José Sandoval and Manuel Azcárate, *Spain, 1936-1939* (London, 1963), pp. 125-149.

108. For the role of Franco during World War II, see Allen Chase, *Falange: The Axis Secret Army in the Americas* (New York, 1943), *passim;* Foltz, *op. cit., passim;* Herbert Feis, *The Spanish Story* (New York, 1948), *passim;* Emmet John Hughes, *Report from Spain* (New York, 1947), pp. 229-274; Thomas J. Hamilton, *Appeasement's Child, The Franco Regime in Spain* (New York, 1943), *passim;* Sir Samuel Hoare (Lord Templewood), *Complacent Dictator* (New York, 1947), *passim;* Juan Negro, *Españoles en la URSS* (Madrid, 1959), *passim; Pasaremos,* pp. 266-275; Ansaldo, *op. cit.,* pp. 250-344; Donald S. Detwiler, *Hitler, Franco und Gibraltar, Die Frage des Spanischen Eintritts in den Zweiten Weltkrieg* (Wiesbaden, 1962), *passim.*

For the contributions of Spanish Republicans to the Allied Victory, see Antonio Vilanova, *Los Olvidados, Los Exilados Españoles en la Segunda Guerra Mundial.* Paris, 1969. As this volume goes to press, a revised version of my *Struggle for Madrid* is being published in Spanish as *El Asedio de Madrid* Paris, 1970.